Golf

How to Play With Confidence From the Sand

(Unabashedly Honest Golf Tips for the Unitiated and Clueless)

Marisa Marcum

Published By **Andrew Zen**

Marisa Marcum

All Rights Reserved

Golf: How to Play With Confidence From the Sand (Unabashedly Honest Golf Tips for the Unitiated and Clueless)

ISBN 978-1-77485-524-9

No part of this guidebook shall be reproduced in any form without permission in writing from the publisher except in the case of brief quotations embodied in critical articles or reviews.

Legal & Disclaimer

The information contained in this ebook is not designed to replace or take the place of any form of medicine or professional medical advice. The information in this ebook has been provided for educational & entertainment purposes only.

The information contained in this book has been compiled from sources deemed reliable, and it is accurate to the best of the Author's knowledge; however, the Author cannot guarantee its accuracy and validity and cannot be held liable for any errors or omissions. Changes are periodically made to this book. You must consult your doctor or get professional medical advice before using any of the suggested remedies, techniques, or information in this book.

Upon using the information contained in this book, you agree to hold harmless the Author from and against any damages, costs, and expenses, including any legal fees potentially resulting from the application of any of the information provided by this guide. This disclaimer applies to any damages or injury caused by the use and application, whether directly or indirectly, of any advice or information presented, whether for breach of contract, tort, negligence, personal injury, criminal intent, or under any other cause of action.

You agree to accept all risks of using the information presented inside this book. You need to consult a professional medical practitioner in order to ensure you are both able and healthy enough to participate in this program.

Table of Contents

INTRODUCTION 1

Chapter 1: The 15 Most Common Faux-Pas That Beginners All Make 4

Chapter 2: Mind Over Matter 12

Chapter 3: Separation In The Preparation 18

Chapter 4: Swing Setup In Five Simple Steps 28

Chapter 5: Put & Chipping 42

Chapter 6: Course Management Like The Pros .. 52

Chapter 7: Golf At An Professional Level: What Exactly Is It? 59

Chapter 8: Improve Your Swing At Golf To The Next Step (Expert) 66

Chapter 9: Contact With The Expert Level Golf Ball 73

Chapter 10: Training For Golf: Mental Strength 80

Chapter 11: Putting Stroke: Expert Level 88

Chapter 12: How Can A Golf Teacher Assist You In Your Professional Level? 95

Chapter 13: Practice Drills 103

Chapter 14: Tours For Golfers Of The Expert Level: And Tournaments 111

Chapter 15: Water Golf Is An Unforgettable Experience 118

Chapter 16: Golf Technology For Professional-Level Players 123

Chapter 17: Golf Tips 131

Chapter 18: Preowned Golf Equipment A Perfect Option 161

Chapter 19: Golf Swing 170

Conclusion 182

Introduction

Golf is a sport which is about scoring the correct numbers. The correct numbers are low numbers, and the higher score is determined by the level of your ability. This desire for low numbers and less error that bring golfers back again and again. Professional golfers will find that the numbers are staggeringly low. Every professional golfer would like to achieve a 59 in their entire career. In major championships, the most desirable number is 62. While many golfers have managed to shoot at least of 63 at major championships but no one has achieved a 62- which makes this number a mythical goal that's waiting to be achieved.

Of course it's true that to the typical golfer, figures like the mid-60's (or even the 50's) are just an imagined scenario. But this doesn't mean that amateur golfers don't set specific goals in terms of numbers that they have set for themselves. One goal common to millions of golfers across the globe is breaking 90 on the 18-hole course. The ability to score a score in the 80's, or anywhere in the 80's is something that many golfers have been up all in the night thinking about. If you've spent the majority of your time playing golf scores in the 1990's or low 100's, the thought of making it to the 80's may seem to be not even possible.

However, this isn't the case. If you're able to score some marks from the early 90's then you already have the ability to score a score during the 1980's. Although you may think you have to completely alter your swing to get that score it is actually only necessary to make some minor adjustments to your plan of attack and technique. Simply by adjusting your current actions doing when you play golf it's possible to cut the remaining strokes from your scores.

The information contained in this book has all the details that you require to bring your scores into the 80's. As you've already figured out, just reading a book going to the next tee isn't going to let you achieve your targets. Instead, you'll need to be able to comprehend the concepts below to implement it effectively. There is no one who is able to play better golf than you. It's your responsibility to follow the instructions and implement it at the driving range and at the golf course. Only when you play an active part in your own development can you overcome that magical 90-degree barrier. Don't waste time now, let's begin to transform you into the golfer you think you could be!

Chapter 1: The 15 Most Common Faux-Pas That Beginners All Make

The golfers on the course are not identical, yet a large number of them commit the same mistakes. If you went to any golf course at all on an overcrowded Saturday morning you'd be able to see a variety identical mistakes made by each player as groups move through. These mistakes are easy to avoid, yet , the majority of amateur players do not spend the time to get rid of these mistakes out of their games. If you are able to eliminate the basic mistakes listed that follow from your game of golf, you'll be one step closer to achieving scores in the 80's.

#1 - Picking the wrong Tees

If you're a high handicap golfer, you've no right to be at the back of the tees of an extended golf course. It is important to select the right set of tees which is suitable for your current level of skill in the present. If you're a player who's not yet break 90, you should look at a distance between 6,000 and 6,500 yards. This variety of yards can allow you to test yourself without presenting an unattainable task.

#2 - Obsessing Over Distance

The distance you drive from does not matter as much as you believe it does. Does it help to drive the ball long from the tee? Yes, but it's not as efficient as hitting the ball directly through the fairway hole, holes after holes. Make sure you are focusing on the accuracy of distance to take playing to the next stage.

#3 - Automatically aiming for the Driver

When it comes to distance, some golfers are so concerned over hitting their ball in a far distance that they immediately go for the driver at the tee of each par four or five. This is an error. When playing shorter holes holes that have many hazards to be concerned about, don't be scared to strike a shorter club, with the intention of putting the ball into the play in a safe manner.

#4 - Ignoring Lag Putting

The ability to put the ball down with two putts to the green is essential for breaking 90. If you're looking to bring your score to the 80's, you don't want to waste strokes three-putting. So, it is essential to get your speed dialed perfect at the beginning of your round. If you can manage your speed, you'll be capable of keeping the greens for three puts off your scorecard.

#5 - You are the only player on the Course

Golf is fun and it's tempting to grab every opportunity to take a trip to the course. But there's a lot to learn at the driving range hitting balls to practice. When you turn some of your golf time into practice time at the range, you'll improve your game over the long haul.

#6 - Try to Buy an Improved Game

It's true that high-end equipment can be a game changer on the field. However, it will only achieve a certain amount. If you believe you're likely to continue buying more clubs until you hit your goal of scoring and you're going to end up dissatisfied and broken. Make a set of nice clubs and change your focus to improving your mental and physical game to break off that 90-degree barrier.

#7 - In the Air

A lot of amateurs believe that the only method to make a golf shot is to hit your ball up as far into the air as is possible. There are plenty of fantastic shots that can be crafted when you keep the ball near to the ground while it is flies towards the goal. Find out how to control low shots, and you'll have more options of shots that you can use in accordance with the conditions and the layout on the field.

#8 - Not able to find the Short Side

This is the typical rookie error. The green's side that is where the hole is can be referred to as the short side. Missing your approach shot from this green can be an ideal way to create the mistake of making a bogey or worse. Make a habit of shooting your approach shots towards the wide end of the green, so you'll be able to make a better chip should you happen to not hit the hole. This method requires patience as you'll be aiming a little off the green however, it can help you reduce strokes later on.

#9 - Playing any Old Golf Ball

Your choice of golf club you select matters a lot - in fact it could be even more than the clubs you use. You must choose the best golf ball for the speed of your swing and shorter game preferences. There is no need to purchase the highest priced ball available however, you must take the time to study various models until you discover one that fits your game. After you've picked one, you should stick to it until you have an understanding of the model.

#10 - Compounding Mistakes

In the par 72 course, all you need to do is to score 17 bogeys and one par in order to reach your goal of getting to 90. In this way, the problem isn't that difficult. Why are so many players come up short? They repeat their mistakes on the hole, and can result in several double bogeys, or even worse. If you make a poor golf shot in a hole do not attempt to create the perfect shot with the next shot to make up for. Instead, select a safe spot and take a calculated shot to get the ball back to its proper position. Being patient enough to keep from hitting huge numbers is a major aspect of this game.

#11 - Speeding through the Golf Swing

From a technical standpoint Many players are quick to complete their golf swing and do not allow the golf club to be in the proper position. There's no rush in your swing since the ball won't be able to disappear prior to hitting it. Be patient in the backswing to put your body into a good posture, then unleash the club as it descends into the strike.

#12 - Not Taking the short Game

It's not as enjoyable to practice chipping and pitching skills as it is to get used to hitting your driver However, these pitches and chips could save you a few strokes while playing. Make time to practice and improve your game on the green and anticipate your scores to start falling quickly.

#13 - Losing Perspective

The ultimate goal could consist of breaking the 90 mark but your main focus on the course must be on hitting each shot to the highest of your ability. If your mind is occupied by the thought of breaking 90 when you're playing the first hole, you'll not be able to perform the potential you have. Concentrate on each swing, and make sure to wait until the time is up to count them all.

#14- Fighting Your Ball Flight

The majority of golfers who shoot in the 90's aren't equipped with the ability to alter their ball's trajectory based on the hole they're playing. If you're in this category, it's fine - you simply have to accept those limitations, and remain to the shot you are confident you are able to make. If, for instance, your usual shot is a huge fade, make sure you plan each shot to allow the fade to take effect. It doesn't matter if the shot is beautiful, as long as the ball ends towards the intended target.

#15 - Accusing Oneself to Pressure

Even if you're not tracking your score precisely throughout the course, you'll be aware in your head when you've had an excellent round. If that's the case it is essential to keep your cool and continue to make good swings throughout the hole that is the last. Making 90 is as mentally as it is physically and you must control the pressure effectively during the final few holes if you want be able to reach this amazing landmark.

Chapter 2: Mind Over Matter

The mental aspect of golf can be intriguing as well as extremely frustrating. Being able to control your thoughts when you're playing golf could reduce your strokes at the finish of the round with more effective decision-making and better performance under stress. There are numerous factors that affect the mental aspects of golf. Educating yourself about how your mental game operates is the first step to improve your performance.

Be sure to test your Temper on the 1st Tee

Golfers are known for throwing temper tantrums while playing that may include throwing clubs or bag kicks, as well as more than just a handful of four-letter words. While it's entertaining to witness another person get angry for a short time but you shouldn't repeat the same mistake. If you let your temper get to out of control at the course likely greatly hinder the chances of you achieving your goals in scoring. If you're determined to getting to 90, you must keep your temper in the house to concentrate all your attention on the job that is at hand.

Does this mean you're not able to get angry when playing golf? Absolutely not. Try to convince yourself that you aren't annoyed at times is naive and untrue. Golf is a tough game and you're likely to be annoyed with yourself when you make an error. It's okay to feel frustrated but it's not acceptable to carry your anger onto another shot. The job of golfer is to manage your emotions in a timely manner so that you can let them go when you are ready to move in the course. When you allow your anger from your previous shot influence the next shot it could lead you into a direction that will cost you a lot of strokes before you're back to where you started.

The well-tested method of counting up to ten when dealing with anger is a great strategy in golf. If you miss a bad shot, you should allow yourself to be angry for a period of ten minutes before "dumping" all the frustration and moving to the next. If you are able to adhere to this principle throughout your game then you can remove your temper from the list things to be enhanced within your sport.

Designing Games Plan

In any other sport there is a game plan. It is something that's expected and sometimes even mandatory. For instance the football team will not play the game on a Sunday without having a game plan. The game plan determines the decisions of coaches and players in their quest to take on the opposing team.

There may not be a team facing you when arrive on the golf course, but the course itself could be viewed as an opponent. Like the football team creates an approach to play in response to their opponents, so do you create your game plan around the course you're playing. The best strategy for a course that is wide and flat is not applicable to courses that are hilly and tree-lined. Therefore, taking the time to modify your game plan prior to each round is crucial. Before starting your round, you need to determine how often you're going to drive your driver, which direction of ball you're likely to choose, and the level of aggressiveness you're going to be in your shot-making.

The key to success in a game plan is total and complete trust in your plan prior to when you begin putting it into practice. Any doubts you are experiencing about your play style will be evident in the course. For example, if you choose to play with a hefty degree of aggression but aren't confident enough about the swing of your game to let the strategy work, the result is certain to disappoint. Choose a strategy and play that you're sure of and are sure to succeed.

Finding the balance between fun and focus

One of the challenges of playing the game mentally for golfers who are not professionals is managing the need to concentrate on the work at hand and having fun with friends while doing it. The game of golf is meant to be a fun activity and you should be able to laugh with your golfing buddies as you progress through the course. Professional golfers will find this job is straightforward and easy since they are paid to make the best scores they can. There's no need to be a social person and they can concentrate all their efforts on playing top golf.

It is, however, possible to be a good player while still maintaining the social aspect that is a part of playing. The key is the ability to manage time. In a four-hour game of golf you'll only swing the club for about a few minutes in total. So, there's plenty of time to talk and have fun while you're taking a walk between holes or waiting for your crowd ahead to complete. The most effective way to keep your level of performance and still having fun is to keep your focus to the shot in front enough time to choose the appropriate club, select the right target and hit the ball. In the end, if you focus for only one minute per shot, you'll be able to have an amazing golf game. If you shot 89, it means that you'll need focus for 89 minutes total which is about an hour half. If you're in the course for 4 hours, that's over two hour for having fun with your friends!

In the Game Above Everything Else

It's easy to make golf strategies more complicated than it really needs to be. Golf courses are huge with lots of slopes, hazards, trees, bunkers and more to think about. But there's an simple way to simplify your plan and keep your head focused throughout the course. When you are on the course, you should make it your primary goal to avoid making penalty shots. When you're ready to hit a shot choosing a club and goal, keep the avoidance penalties as your principal goal. So long as you keep the ball in play throughout the 18 holes, you'll have a good chance of succeed in breaking 90.

You'll have to apply a lot of patience when you employ this simple , yet effective technique when playing the golf course. If you're faced with an approach shot that is aimed at the green, which is protected by water, it is important to make it a point to keep your shot clear of the water, even if it means that you are aiming towards the hole. One of the key elements of a golfing strategy is knowing the right time to be aggressive as well as when you should play safe. This decision can be determined by the existence and absence of obstacles that could result in penalties shots. If there's no risk of penalty shots awaiting you near the green, then go ahead and hit the flag. If a small error can leave your shot in hazard of water or even out of the bounds so, you should take the safer option and keep penalty shots off your scorecard. It's hard enough to break 90 and you shouldn't have to add fast adding additional strokes.

Chapter 3: Separation In The Preparation

The way you plan for every round of golf you play tells the extent to which you're hoping to meet your goals. If you arrive at the course at the right time to pay your green fees and then walk straight to the first tee, then you probably don't have a lot of enthusiasm about achieving 90. But if you're determined to arrive early and prepare for the game, you are definitely committed to making the effort to complete the task.

A well-planned warm-up is essential to your success since it is impossible to afford to miss shots in the first couple of holes as you find your own rhythm for the rest of the day. You must start your game with a bang immediately from the first tee shot if wish to be in any chance of making a record-setting personal best. A lot of golfers choose the easy route and do not spend time warming up prior to their round. Afterward, the complain of how badly they're doing to begin the day. Don't be one of these people. The quality of your warm-up will directly affect the standard of your game earlier in the round, so make the work prior to your round if you want to receive high scores.

Diversity in your Warm Up Session

Making a commitment to a complete warm-up is an excellent start however, you must be aware of the things you need to include in your warm-up for you to achieve the most effective outcomes. When golfers do show up on the course before the time they need to get warm, many simply go towards the range to empty the large bucket prior to walking to the first golf course. Although hitting a bucket of balls is superior to hitting anything else but your complete swing is just one aspect in the process. In order to be prepared for when you begin the round, you'll need to be familiar with every aspect that make up the game such as the full swing chipping, putting, and bunker play.

Below is a warm-up routine that you might want to try before your next workout. Of course, you are able to make slight adjustments to this basic outline to ensure it is perfect for your needs.

1. You should arrive one hour prior to the time you'll be playing. You should check into the pro shop immediately and complete any

other obligations during this time (using the bathroom, purchasing an item for snack, etc.).

2. Take a trip to the putting course to practice the speed of greens that you will be playing on. In this moment, you're just focusing at the pace of greens so you should hit long putts in a row on the green you are practicing with for a couple of minutes. There's no need to be concerned about the ability to make putts at this point and you don't have to aim at the hole to practice your putts. The goal is simply to get familiar with the speed or how slow the greens are moving at this time of the year.

3. Proceed to the chipping zone, in the event that one is accessible. Take a variety balls from fairway lie, as well as the rough. Try to make good contact on your shots and choose a target for every shot. It is not necessary to make a lot of chip shots, but just 10 or 15 would suffice. The process of warming up prior to a round isn't the time to focus on improving the technique of your

golfer, so the focus should be on establishing the right chipping pattern to play the round. If the course you're playing has a bunker for practice it is the perfect time to take some warm-up shots from the sand.

4. About 30 minutes prior to your tee-time go to the driving range and play a few balls. It's not a good idea to work on your chipping technique prior to the round is doubled for you to hit the ball with your entire swing. It's not a practice session, so don't think of it as one. The goal of your driving course prior the course is warming your muscles, establish an appropriate pace and gain confidence for the course. Additionally, you do not want to tire yourself to death before you enter the golf course, so try not to make more than you can handle. The exact number you want to be hitting is a matter of individual preference, but anything over 30 is likely to be a challenge for many amateur golfers.

5. Make sure you finish your range time with approximately 15 minutes remaining until the time you tee off. In this moment you'll need go back to the practice green to putt a number of putts that are short. This is the final step before you head on to your first hole. Pick five golf ball from the bag, and put them in a row at least three feet away from a hole. Make five putts and then move them back at least four feet prior to making putts again. Repeat the procedure one more time, starting at five feet. Repeat until you've made fifteen putts in succession. In the final stages of your warm-up practice with a series short putts that are successful can help you increase your confidence in this vital aspect of golf prior to beginning your round.

6. Once you've finished your warm-up take a walk for the first green couple of minutes prior to the time you've scheduled for your tee. It isn't a good idea to rush off the tee to take your first shot quickly So, make sure

you arrive with at most a couple of minutes to be spare.

If you are able to complete the above steps (or equivalent) prior to each round you will be moving towards the proper direction. Golfers who complete an entire warm-up process will be more prepared to play both from the physical and mental standpoint. The mental aspect of the warmup is one which many players do not consider. It is important to warm up before playing an event isn't just focused on getting the muscles prepared to go , it's as well about sharpening your brain to face the challenges ahead. A proper warm-up can increase your confidence and aid in getting into the golf frame of mind.

Nutrition Matters

In addition to the basics of getting you golf stroke and put stroke prepared for the tough demands ahead, you must prepare your body for an 18-hole game of golf, which could take at least four hours. You may not consider golf as physically demanding however, you could easily get tired throughout the day if your body isn't well-nourished. A healthy diet and plenty of fluids plays an important role in preparing you for a successful day at the course.

When choosing an appropriate meal for your dinner, make sure you choose alternatives that are healthy and satisfying. Of course, your personal preferences and tastes will dictate the food items you choose to consume prior to your round, but you should avoid foods that are too oily or sweet. You need to provide your body the fuel it needs to get through the day and avoid stomach discomfort that can follow you around the course. Alongside eating well prior to the start of your round it is important to carry an extra snack or two snacks in your bag for when you require an extra boost of energy on the way.

A further aspect of warming up is to drink plenty of fluids. Although this advice is applicable to everyone but it's especially crucial in the event that you will be playing on a very hot day. Start your game with plenty of fluids in your system. Then, continue to drink fluids while on the course. You could substitute for a sports drink, if you want, but you should make sure you stay away from alcohol or soda, as they'll just hinder your quest to achieve that magical sub-90 mark.

Make sure to check your equipment

The final part of the warm-up puzzle is an inspection in your bags to ensure that you have everything you require to play the course. Things like golf balls, tees and gloves can be bought at last minute from the pro shop therefore, make a list in your bags and add the items that are running low. It's always better to be prepared rather than unprepared, so pack an extra set of items in case your round doesn't go as you expected it to. For instance, you could believe that five or six tees are sufficient, but you could be on the course and realize that you're not hitting a tee on every shot. Make sure your bag is well-stocked with all the necessary items to ensure that there are no problems to be faced after the round is over.

In the end the most important thing is that a great warm-up session should make you feel confident and ready for the next round. It is possible that your typical initial tee-jitters have diminished and may even disappear after an efficient warm-up. It's true that you need to spend a little time and effort into the warm-up process to ensure that you do the right thing however, the sacrifices will be worthwhile when you're finally able to write your score on the 18th hole, which begins with an "8".

Chapter 4: Swing Setup In Five Simple Steps

The golf swing starts before you move the club. When you walk up to the ball and stand you must be mindful of how you execute your plan. You must be in the right place and place your body in properly and be in the right mindset to make good shots. If you choose to take a more relaxed approach to preparing your shots, you're likely to fail frequently. Consistency is among the main requirements when you are thinking about hitting 90 first time and you can dramatically increase your consistency through the round by setting up properly.

To become proficient with the swing follow the five step procedure each time you take the ball. While these five steps may appear to be a lot of work to complete prior to each shot, with just a amount of practice, you'll be able complete the five steps within few minutes.

Step One - Positioning Your Feet

The first step of your preparation should be to ensure that your feet are in the correct place. It is vital to position your feet in a proper way before hitting any shot in golf, since the distance you stand from the ball will determine the kind of swing you are able to execute. To ensure you're at the right space from your ball and your arms are hanging free from your shoulders when you take your position. Put the club's head in front of the ball, allowing your arms to float freely after placing your hands in the club's grip and you are capable of putting your feet properly in accordance with the hand position. You should feel comfortable with the way your feet are in place on the ground, and you shouldn't feel as if you're reaching out to grab the club. But, at the same time you should not feel like you're affluent on the ball. Take some time to practice your posture in the course until you're able to put your feet at the right space from the ball each time.

Step Two Step Two - Flex Your knees

When your feet are in the proper place and your feet in the right position, the next step of this process would be to create some flex into your knees. It is crucial to keep your knees in a flex position because it will enable your lower body part to assume an energetic role in the downswing. This is precisely what you wish to accomplish. After taking your position, bend your knees several times to stretch your legs. Also, make sure your muscles are primed to swing the shot that is soon to begin. The ideal amount of knee flex differ from one person to the next and so you should try different levels of flexibility until you have settled at the ideal amount to swing at. If you're having trouble getting your legs into the proper position consider sitting in an armchair while you are flexing your knees. The same movement you make when you sit down - putting your backside in front of you - is ideal to help you get into the perfect golf position.

Third Step - Aligning the Shoulder

After two steps the lower body should be prepared to move. You're in a good posture, as well as your knees bent at the correct angle. The next step is to examine the posture on your shoulder. Ideally, you want to make sure that your shoulders are square to the line of your target in line with the line drawn through your foot. If you start your swing with your shoulders closed or open to the line formed through your feet you'll add unnecessary complexity in your swing. It is best to get your shoulders roughly in line with the target line when hitting So starting off in that position will help simplify the swing's overall motion. If you're unable to tell the position of your shoulders when you practice and adjusting them, have a friend verify for they can tell where you are. If the line drawn by your shoulders lines up with the line made by your feet you're now in good shape to go and complete step 4.

Step Four - Make Sure You Keep Your Head Up

Maintaining your chin in the right position is the second most important element to the puzzle of setup. Most golfers will make the error of putting their chins down to their chests, which makes it extremely difficult to make an entire turn on the backswing. The goal is for your left shoulder to move underneath your chin when you are in the backswing. That can only occur when your chin is raised when you are at the address. While you must keep your eye focused on your ball however, that doesn't mean that you shouldn't keep your head in the same direction. Keep your head straight while your eyes are closed, and you'll be in a good position to swing your club quickly.

Step Five: A Deep Breath

The final step of getting ready to hit the golf ball is to breathe deeply. It may not be something that is crucial however, a slow and deep breath will go a long way in relaxing your muscles before you begin the swing. Take this breath as an opportunity to take your time and organize your mind to strike the shot you're trying to hit. Being able to play well golf and eventually hitting 90, will require a clear head before every swing, and taking a deep breath can help get your mind in an ideal position.

As we've mentioned the five steps may appear to be a lot of work to accomplish initially. You definitely don't want to spend five minutes to get ready for every swing, so you'll have to figure out how to cross off the five items listed in minutes. This is why the driving range is crucial for your success. If you focus on these five steps at the driving range in every practice session, they'll become automatic to you. In reality, after several sessions on the range you will notice that you're completing the steps without contemplating the steps. This is the objective - being able to put the ball in a 'autopilot' and your mind is completely focused on the ball and execute the swing.

It is crucial to get the ball set up right on all of your shots, none is more vital than when you're striking the driver. Because the driver is the longest club you have in you bag, all errors made with drivers will be magnified. For instance, if, for example, you strike your pitching wedge while keeping the face slightly away from the line of your target the shot will drift just a bit to the left (for the right-handed player). If you do not leave your driver's face that is open by a couple of degrees and the ball will end up a bit to the right of the goal. Any mistakes can be magnified by hitting the ball for 250 yards or more. So, make sure you get the specifics of your driver's setup correct every time.

The ability to hit the ball with accuracy is one of the main aspects of breaking 90. If you can put the ball on the green from every tee and take care not to miss any penalties along the way, then you'll have the best chance to score at the top of the range in the 1980's. In reality it isn't necessary to play the fairway every hole if you take an opportunity to look at the green when you are preparing your shot. The rough isn't a problem on the majority of golf courses, however you should be in a place where you are able to aim your shot at the green, instead of being forced to lay-up. Golfers who can consistently drive their ball straight and long have an advantage over players who are playing from trees throughout the day.

The five steps for setting up above are applicable to the driver the same way as they do for the other clubs you have. In addition to the setup suggestions there are additional things you can do to improve your driving. Follow these tips to get to the longest and accurate drives of your life.

* Make sure to take a second to the top. Many amateur golfers speed up their backswing along with their driver, because they are in an euphoria to smash the ball as hard as they can. If you are really looking to smash your drives in the middle, you'll need to allow some extra time on your backswing. By adding an additional 'beat' towards the top of the swing, you will be able to gather your thoughts and get ready

for a fast turn towards the goal. The timing is crucial in golf swings, and you'll see an improvement in the accuracy of your shots by taking a longer for the swing to take shape.

Pick the safest lines. It is unlikely that you will be able to let your driver loose completely off the tee if worry of hitting it into a danger or out of the bounds. If you're looking to hit your best shots start with picking safe routes from the tee. Make sure you are aiming away from danger to the wider part of fairway even if it requires an approach shot that is longer. The aim is to locate the grass that is short and allow yourself to have a shot when you take your next swing. There's no way to make excellent approach shots if your ball is located at the bottom of the lake, so you must concentrate on driving drives that hit the fairway. It's not as thrilling to choose most secure targets, but if the intention will be to hit 90 or more, this is exactly what you ought to be doing.

* Refrain from doing something. It's true, one of the most effective ways to improve driving is to strike the ball at around 90 percent of your max effort. Even if you plan to send the ball straight across the fairway on the par 5 but you must keep something in order to maintain control and stability. If you are swinging with all your might, it is sure to cause you to fall off balance and it's impossible to make good shots when your body weight is not in the right place. Take a step back with every shot if want to achieve the consistency needed to achieve your highest score.

The advice in this chapter ought to be all you need to get started playing consistently good golf during a round. Make sure to keep the game simple and concentrate on the setup, not the movements of your swing. As long as your technique is sound on the technical side and you have the best chance of getting the ball in the vicinity of the goal. Be aware that perfection isn't achievable on the golf course ; it's all about consistent, solid shots that will keep you from trouble and on track to get the ultimate score of 90 (or higher).

THE SWING

1. Ball Position

The spine of your body is tilted just a slightly to the right, while your body weight is equally dispersed. This is crucial for the correct mechanics during the swing. Your ball's location is on your left foot. Be sure to bend your knees.

2. Begin to Backswing

The hands, hips and shoulders and arms all begin to turn and move simultaneously. Keep your left arm straight. The wrists will break slightly to let the club slide through your back.

3. The top of the Backswing

The club should be locked 90 degrees towards the left side of your arm. The right knee should be moved out a bit and this will let the left thigh stretch and then move towards the ball. This is the traditional power position. It can prepare you for the downswing's transition.

4. The Downswing

The left heel is replanted. The left leg is ready to take the swing that is coming forward. The separation between your shoulders and hips lets you maintain an angle of 90 degrees between the shaft of the club along with your arm. Your core is still in front of the golf ball, your hips are moving, and the shoulders remain locked.

5. Coming Down

Turn your shoulders and chest with your shoulders, but keeping the 90-degree angle between you and the shaft of the club. Use your legs to drive up. Your hips should be turning and drive your left shoulder back and up. It is important to feel like the body and the club's weight are moving across the contact zone.

6. Follow Through

Let you to allow the force of your head and head of the club to drag you through the swing. Your weight will continue to shift as you turn. The belt buckle must be looking towards the direction of your shot. You're now in a position where you can watch the shot glide through the middle of the fairway.

Chapter 5: Put & Chipping

The majority of amateur golfers prefer to work at the driving range and hitting balls after balls in search that perfect shot. Of course, you'll be aware that there isn't a thing as an ideal golf swing. If you're spending most of your time practicing hitting balls, you're losing a massive chance to improve your game. While it is crucial to refine how you swing your club, it's essential to develop your short game abilities. It may be fun to throw the ball to the sky as high as it is possible to, but it's much more enjoyable to roll into a birdie putt, or hit a perfect back and forth save to get par. To make it to 90 first time your short game must been up to the task. A well-constructed golf swing can't be achieved without a short game that matches.

One reason that players tend to do not practice the game that is short is that it doesn't appear to need the same amount of practice as the longer game. The full swing is a complex series of well-coordinated moves which can be performed at speeds of 100 miles an hour and more. In the context of contract, putting and chipping seem to be fairly simple. It doesn't require you to be able to swing with force or perform full turns to make a perfect chip or putt. But, despite the apparent ease of playing golf's short games, it's really difficult to master. There are numerous tiny details to playing the game of short that need to be learned through constant training. You cannot hit just chip and putt and expect a good performance the best short game needs to be learned through hundreds of repetitions.

The physical aspect in the shorter game could be learned by spending a lot of time playing in the short-game practice area on your local golf course. By practicing your short game on a regular basis with a focus on some basic rules, you will be able to increase your physical ability within a short period of time. But, this practice will not help how you think about playing the short game, which could be more crucial. For the most out of your short game playing, you're going to require a solid mental game plan, which requires one thing: visualization. Visualizing your shots can be powerful, yet the majority of golfers do not even attempt it. If you are able to incorporate visualization into your game with success it is possible to chip your shots further and make more putts in the near future.

Visualizing Your Putts

Visualization can be a fantastic method to boost efficiency on the green for putting. If you're just strolling towards the ball and hitting a shot you can greatly improve your putting in the process of visualizing the ball moving towards the hole before you hit the ball. It is essential to know the level of commitment needed to see your putts in a correct manner every hole. Visualization isn't something you can just do with a little zeal You must commit to the visualization of your putts to achieve a great outcome. The majority of professionals employ some kind of visualization while playing, and you should use the same method.

In order to incorporate visualization into your routine of putting follow these simple steps listed below.

1. Before you begin any sort of visualization it is essential to be able to read the putt you are looking at. Make sure to study the putt from various angles. Then, you can choose an exact direction and speed you'll make use of to get the putt. For instance, it's not adequate to claim that you will putt a bit to the left in the middle of your hole'. Instead, you must choose to target six inches to the left and 2 feet in length'. This means you're going to hit the ball for six inches and then hit the ball with enough velocity to move two feet over to the hole (unless it hits the hole). The process of visualizing will not be effective without a specific reading, so don't cut the corners when it comes to this aspect of the procedure.

2. Once you have your reading in place Now you are able to begin the process of

visualizing. At this moment you should be approximately five feet from the ball. You should be looking directly at the hole, and your ball lying on the green in front of you. hole. Keep your eyes focused at the ball, follow a route to the hole with your eyes, following the direction of your reading. When you look in this imaginary line imagine the ball rolling on the ground. Your visualization should be as precise as you can. Watch the ball take the break before falling to the bottom of the cup.

3. After you've thought of the putt from the back then walk towards the ball and then take your position. When your body is set, turn your eyes towards the hole and visualize the final several feet a second time. It is not advisable to imagine the whole putt while standing on top of the ball since your body may become tense at this point. Take a look to the golf hole and look up the last few feet, and imagine the ball rolling into the hole again. Once you have returned your eyes toward the ball begin

your stroke straight away. Sitting still in front of the ball only gives your brain time to play so be sure to avoid any doubt and begin your stroke when your eyes are positioned on the ball.

If you're the first time using techniques of visualization in golf, then you may be amazed at how effective they can be. If done properly, you'll think you've watched the ball enter the hole before and the actual putt is just an rerun of the event. However, this is only effective if you believe in the method. Be confident on the strength of visualisation, and you will soon begin to putt more.

Another important thing to remember when clarified it's that one doesn't need to envision the ball hitting the hole. For instance, if you are making the putt from 100 feet away, which is on the other edge of the green making the putt isn't an ideal target. In this case you'll would like to imagine the ball moving to within a few inches of your hole in order to create a tap.

Visualizing Your Chip Shots

The method for visualization of your chips is identical to the procedure described above to visualize your putts. In fact, you could apply the same outline, but with one important change. Instead of picturing the ball flying all through the hole wish to imagine the chip shot as it is flying in the air. The only thing you can control with the chip shot is the distance at which the ball is able to fly through the air, and the path it follows to get there. After the ball bounces and rolls, it'll depend on the reading of the green's direction to carry the ball all the way.

If you are walking up to the green, and realize that you'll chip, the first step is to read of the green, just as when you put. It is crucial to study the green with care prior to making chipping because a large portion of the distance for the shot will be covered by the ground. Check the break of the ground as well as the total distance you'll have to cover in order to hit the shot. After you've got that info you can return to the ball to figure out the specifics of your chip shot. There are several variables to think about when you chip, for instance the following:

• What type of lie are you in? If you're playing from a bad lying position, you'll prefer for the ball to be as low to the ground you can. If you are playing from a great lying position, you'll be able to launch the ball higher to the sky on higher speed.

* What's the state that the turf is in? A shot with soft conditions is one which flies the majority of route to the target as hard and dry turf lets you play an eagle and run.

* Which club do you prefer to choose? A majority of players have a favourite club they make the majority the chip shots. What club is best is right for you? It's okay to choose one club for chipping over the others, as long as you are able to utilize it in various scenarios.

If you're lucky, you'll be able to swiftly decide on the kind of chip you will make. Once you have your reading in mind and the type of chip shot chosen the next step is to select the location of your landing for your shot. The landing point is perhaps the most crucial aspect of your chip shot because the place where the ball hits will ultimately determine where it will land at the hole. Find the spot you think will allow the ball to bounce off and roll towards the hole.

This is where visualization is crucial. When you've chosen your landing area you can stand in front of the ball, and imagine the shot flying across the sky and landing precisely at that location. It's not necessary to imagine the remainder of the shot. Simply imagine the ball bouncing from the golf club, and landing perfectly at the spot you have chosen. When you've completed your visualization you can walk to the ball and then hit exactly the shot you imagined in your head.

Improved performance when chipping or putting can be the quickest way to break the 90-degree barrier. You can save a huge amount of strokes by having an better short game - far more than you could save by adjusting your swing. Make use of visualization in your chipping and putting game and a score of the 80's could be right around the corner.

Chapter 6: Course Management Like The Pros

The way you swing the golf club isn't the only method to reduce your scores. If you are able to improve the way you manage your course it is possible to cut a few strokes off your score without having to change a part of your swing. Course management is often not thought of as a way to improve golf, however it's exactly as crucial as your stance and grip. The right decisions can lead to great swings and the reverse is true. Learn to navigate your golf swing as a professional and you'll be sure to score higher scores, including making 90 in the course for the first time.

The concept of managing the course is no different from game planning for other games. Similar to how the football team has an approach to defeat their opponents, so is it necessary to have an approach to game planning to beat your opponent your golf course. The course plays defense throughout the day with things such as trees, bunkers, the water, many more. To stop this defense, you need be prepared with a plan to follow.

One of the most difficult aspects regarding good course management is that it cannot be replicated from another participant. You must create your course management plan entirely on your own since it's particular to the capabilities you have. Consider, for instance, you're a player who is consistently hitting the ball straight, but don't have much distance from the starting line. If you have that kind of profile it is necessary to adopt a different strategy from someone who can blast the ball over massive distances using the driver. The player could choose to play all of the par fives with two shots, but you might prefer to play cautiously and putting your ball on the short grass. To be at your best you must remain committed with your game and develop plans around your top strengths.

Identify Your Best Approach Distance

The first step in the course management process is to determine the yardage you will use as the number you use for your approaches, as often as you can. It is a number that will allow you to hit your favorite golf club to the green, hoping to create a birdie putt. For example, if like hitting your 9-iron and you are able to hit that club 140 yards in normal conditions, then you'll indicate 140 as your ideal distance for your approach. When you are selecting club off of the green, or deciding on layup yardages you'll always be looking for the 140 mark. Naturally, you'll have your number will be unique your own, therefore take a moment to think about the short iron you prefer and then try to set up as many opportunities with this club as you can.

If you are able, it would be beneficial to determine two distinct yards that you could use to set goals in the fairway. One of them is between 100 to 160 yards and another that's within 100 yards. The smaller number is most often used for par 5s when laid up or on shorter par fours. The higher number is, however is utilized for long or medium par fours. With two numbers you'd be content to play with you'll have more options to design your course management plan.

Always Uphill

The most important rule in the course is that you should be playing uphill. When you are deciding on targets during the day, you must be aware that you're trying to put the ball lower than the hole. Uphill play gives you more control when compared to playing downhill. So, put your shot on the lower side of the golf course as much as you can during the day.

This is especially crucial when you are playing long-distance shots on the green. If you're hitting into the green from more than 175 yardsaway, odds of hitting a perfect shot directly at the desired target are quite low. In this regard, you must choose the best line to place your ball in the hole for your next shot. Even when you do miss the green, you'll play an upward chip, and you'll have a decent chance of getting up and down to keep your par. If you fail on the higher side, you'll face a difficult chip and a bogey could be a possibility.

The goal is 89.

The whole point in this guide is to teach you the necessary skills to shoot 90, it makes sense to create your game strategy that has shooting 89 as your goal. While it is possible to shoot further than that level, beginning with the goal to shoot for 89 would be a good strategy to make intelligent decisions throughout the course. When you make your decisions based on attempting to shoot 89, you'll be able to avoid making mistakes that could end in costing you a number of strokes.

Below are a few suggestions on what you need to do to shoot an 89-

* Assuming that you are playing on a course that is par 72 it is possible to score 17 more than par and still achieve your objective.

This means you can make one par, and still achieve an 89! A round consisting of just one par, and 17 birdies could suffice to complete the task.

Penalty shots can cause you to lose your chance. When you're putting together your course management plan take note of the areas on the course that could be prone be a source of penalty shots to your score, and try to stay clear of them as far as you can. Even if you must deliberately miss the green on an approach shot secured by water, it is better off chipping rather than would be taking a drop of the danger.

* Three putts are the devil of hitting 90 first time. In any game of golf you're likely to make some bad shots. It's inevitable. To maintain your score at the level you want it to be, try to avoid putting three greens. Putt your shots at an easiness so that you are able to leave yourself with easy tap-ins after the second. This is part of the course managing - choosing to make your putts

conservatively in order to avoid the risk of a three putt.

* Removing the driver at times is a smart idea. Like we said earlier it is possible to have a number of bogeys, and still shoot an 89. With this in mind you might consider not hitting the driver on long par fours instead of hitting fairway woods or hybrids off the starting point. This will enable your ball to remain in play even if you must take three shots to get to the green. This strategy could result in the possibility of a bogey but will prevent you from putting up an enormous score that would completely ruin the chances of making it into the 80's.

Professional golfers have a plan for managing their course that they follow when heading to the course for a round and you should do the same. While you might be to play in the 80's rather than from the 1960's, the concept is the same: make wise choices that will give you the best chances of success.

Chapter 7: Golf At An Professional Level: What Exactly Is It?

Gary Player: "The harder you train and work at it, the more luck you have."

Like many other sports, lets you reach higher levels of performance as long as you practice regularly. To be able to get between intermediate and expert there are a lot of factors to pay attention to. For instance, you'll need to pay greater focus on your fairway shots as well as improve your putting skills by learning to control the speed and force that you're striking the ball.

From a practical perspective an objective point of view from a practical point of view, the score is one that defines the difference from an experienced and a pro golfer. Therefore even if you've achieved proficiency in golf at an intermediate level, you should not put off practicing. You must continue to practice in as many and often as you can and to reduce the score and develop your skills. Every now and then it is not a bad idea to return to the basics of the game by paying particular attention to your posture and grip quality good posture, and proper alignment.

It is not likely that you would think you can improve your game , however, when it comes to golf, there's always the possibility of improvement. What you need to do is get out in the practice area or on the course and work on the shots that are the most crucial (such for the shorter game as an instance). It is advised to put in lots of effort to increase your chipping and putting as they account for around 40 percent in the sport. The last, but certainly not least understanding the green is an important aspect even at the professional levels. Being able to manage your speed when playing green can help you improve your game, so be sure you remember this.

If you talk with any experienced or professional golfer they'll immediately inform you that anyone could become an expert in golf. The requirement is to complete at minimum 10.000 hours of training, whether at golf ranges or even on the course. That's why, it's not enough just to imagine being an expert golfer. You need to actually work hard and endure the process, which may turn out to be challenging occasionally. It could take some time to attain the status of expert , but at the end of the day it will be worth it.

At the professional level, efficiency is your primary goal. You may have achieved your best swing, but there's a crucial aspect to be considered and it is control of your swing when you are under stress (as it could happen during an event or contest). Consistency is an essential element of golf at professional levels, and you will need to work hard to build both the necessary reliability and confidence to play at this level.

If you're the practical type, then you are probably aware that playing golf, including levels, is an enormous financial commitment. You must prepare yourself for a significant investment, considering the price of equipment, involvement in different events and tournaments, and the cost of travel and lodging. In addition, you will need an individual coach and you're looking at an enormous investment that you need to be prepared for along with your living expenses. It is always best to establish a strategy about financial matters and to identify who can assist you along the way (for instance, you could draw from your savings or use profits from competitions or tournaments or even locate sponsors).

The length of time is another thing to think about. When you've reached an appropriate stage, you will need to work harder and harder. In addition you'll have to travel a lot particularly if you wish to participate in competitions, tournaments, or other events. Because of this you'll have to give up time that you would otherwise spend at home and with the family. In the event that you're single, you'll need to determine your work schedule or personal passions, as these are sacrifices which have to be made too.

Don't misunderstand golf at professional level with golf at an expert level as they are two distinct things. It's an individual thing to be the best golfer and the other to play to the next level. Professional golfers have a long careerwith a variety of wins and achievements. After an extended period they often turn their focus to the field of teaching or run the golf club or course. Before you begin teaching golf focus on improving your skills.

Talented individuals can aid you in reaching these levels of golf too. This is what experts refer to as natural talent, which you can utilize (and lots of it) in order to improve your golfing skills and abilities. One of the most important attributes is self-confidence, a belief that you are able to achieve more. Being competitive is crucial, since there's a lot of competition. Additionally, you will need to show selfishness occasionally, to get an edge over your competitors.

While it's not an actual quality it can be helpful more than you realize. What is obsession? It is being completely absorbed in the game of golf , and doing it the length of time you want to without getting overwhelmed or being tempted to give up. This is crucial not only for situations where you wish to compete at the highest levels, but as well for those who wish to take it higher and become professional golfers.

As you can see from your own experiences the importance of mental focus is one of the aspects which can be an impact on the outcome of your game. Don't overlook the importance of a solid mentally focused game lightly. If you are too paying attention to things like your posture, grip the swing, stance and more. It is unlikely that you will be able to achieve the same level achievement as you would be able to have with your mental focus.

Food to think about

1.) How do you define the game of golf at an the level of an expert?

2.) Why is it necessary to practice even at this point? Three reasons to consider.

3.) What other traits do you think are beneficial to golf?

Chapter 8: Improve Your Swing At Golf To The Next Step (Expert)

Arnold Palmer: "Concentration comes out of a mix of hunger and confidence."

If you are playing golf your first time you're taught that the swing is the most important thing to master. Although it may seem easy to push the ball into the right direction, time will show you the opposite. As you advance to the next stage in your golfing experience you discover that a great golf swing requires a little sensitivity and a lot of practice. In the advanced level the ability to perfect the golf swing equally vital, and this will allow you to perform at a high level under stress.

Fundamental aspects in the swing of golf

No matter what your current skill level regardless of your current level, there are two important factors that make for the ability to make a decent, or even an excellent swing. One is that you can hit the ball from the tee that is designed to assist you in achieving the highest possible score.

However you must be precise that must be at all times sought. It is crucial to realize that it's never enough to cut down the existing distance (to the green) You must make sure that any mistakes are prevented from happening or else you're bound to fail.

How do you create a longer drive

If you've attained a certain level and have gained many years of knowledge, this isn't a reason to not try to improve your skills and get an extended drive (which can improve your swing too). One of the most important things you should do is to avoid hitting your golf ball using all of the force that you've stored in your body but instead, it's better to focus on your rhythm and maintain it as steady as is feasible. If you are able to keep a steady rhythm you'll notice an increase in your speed (for all shots).

If you are swinging at a rate that is too slow it is possible to change your golf club by choosing one with an easier to move shaft (this will ensure a higher speed of your swings). Don't forget to consider the elements which can impact on your swing. Even the most talented players are "defeated" by certain elements including uneven slopes, the different elevations on the course or the strength of the wind. It is for this reason that it is important to play in various conditions (including the various weather types).

Not last, if you wish to achieve a longer drive, don't alter your stance or posture, particularly if you're playing from rough. You may also wish to be aware of the angle of attack, also known as an angle and the direction of the ball, since they are crucial factors to be considered when you take the swing.

Short game

The basic rule is that if you wish to become an expert at golf, you must master playing short. The bump-and-run shot is very beneficial in situations where you're within a reasonable distance of the hole. It is also referred to as"chip and run" "chip and run" which is an shot that is aimed at the green that is typically is played near an edge on the green. You can throw or chip the ball, based on the conditions and the level of interest.

In addition to trying this type shots, in case are looking enhance your game in the short lane, you could also consider placing your feet more closely together. With high-numbered irons it is recommended to practice chipping from an alternate distance. In addition it is advised to modify your backswing in a similar manner. If you are required to pull the ball away from an trap of sand (or another type of danger in general) it is advised to use the pitching swing, best executed with the aid of a lofted golf club.

It is said that practice makes perfect, and it's a fact that will forever be the golden rule of golf. Making your short game perfect can be achieved only by practicing and, every time you must use each club in a safe way. Don't spend too much time thinking about the longer drive but be aware of other aspects of the game as they could be equally crucial.

Control of Clubface

It is likely that you have been taught about controlling your clubface however we will give a quick overview because this is an important element to be considered. When you are on the downswing, if your clubface is held in a waiting place, then the ball will be left wide. This is certainly not a good idea, since it can result in hitting towards the right of your intended area. However when you try to correct this in the last moment, you'll change the angle of impact, and not be able to complete the entire swing. Therefore, it is important to always remember to control the clubface , and you will strike the ball exactly at the point you want to hit. Be aware of the position of your wrist and arm since they will affect the direction of the club.

Shaft angle (in transition)

Sometimes, regardless of how hard you try to play a decent game, you will fail. If you are discouraged, be aware of the way in which the shaft of your club is situated. Should it be too steep in the middle of your downswing, your entire swing may be affected. It's enough to study professional golfers and observe that they almost always keep their club shaft in a flat, sloping position (at this specific point).

If you do not keep your shaft in the proper place, you could be affecting the face of the club, failing to produce enough velocity for hitting the ball a correct way. Also, you'll be unable to use your body as is required when playing golf. The course of the ball could be affected therefore, make sure you be aware of the angle of the shaft (at the point of change).

Random practice

We've already said that it's an excellent idea to practice in various conditions in order to be ready for all kinds of scenarios (which may be encountered during a crucial event or competition). Random practice is the fact that you're employing a different type of club for each target and every swing you wish to hit or make. However it is recommended to limit the amount of block-practice that is hitting many balls using the same club, and trying to hit the same goal. At this point you're better off by putting your energy into random exercises, as opposed to block-practice.

Final word

Golfers who are experts never ignore that golf can be built on routine. While it's beneficial to play in different conditions, it is equally important to adhere to the same routine when you're on the course. This could be your normal set-up, the positioning of your hands and of course, alignment. It could also be referring the posture you take, posture and even to the placement on the field (or the distance you stand from it).

In certain circumstances it is best to keep your sights on the ball that is, to focus your attention and focus on getting as close to the goal as you can (not making reaching the target your primary goal). If you do fail to hit the target, you'll remain close and thus be satisfied with the shot you've taken. The idea is to set reasonable expectations for each shot you're planning to take.

Food to think about

1.) Are there any other methods to enhance your swing at this point?

2.) Why must we always go back to the basics in the sport?

3.) What makes the practice of randomness more beneficial than block-based practice?

Chapter 9: Contact With The Expert Level Golf Ball

Bobby Jones: "Golf is one of the games in which the ball is positioned poorly and the players play well."

One of the primary aspects taught about golf is the need for a high level of hand-eye coordination. As you grow, you'll surely improve your coordination, however, at times, you will still be difficult to keep a proper connection with the ball. Following the tips included in this chapter you'll definitely be able to achieve the level of expert contact.

Be aware of your grip

It's likely that this has been previously mentioned, but not in any way on how to draw the golf ball. However, if you have an improved grip you will find that it's easier to pull the ball.

Your body should be rotated

Moving your feet around may not be a crucial task, but in reality, it will aid you more than you realize. In the beginning, you must ensure that your feet are closer to each other. This will keep you from sliding and swaying, which is the primary factor that can negatively impact in your equilibrium. In contrast when you get used to rotating your body into position (around middle) and you'll have greater connection with the ball.

Make sure you use the feet safe way

The body's posture and posture will determine whether you're effective in hitting the ball. But, many players even experienced players do not take into consideration the importance of feet. What is the reason feet are so crucial? Because that is where the majority of your control is derived from. If you are able to control your feet, you can also can control your knees. The knees are in control of the hips, and then the hips until the shoulders. In essence in order to make a great connection with the ball it is best to start with your feet. It is suggested to raise the left leg (heel) in the middle of the backswing as this can help you to make an excellent shot.

Be aware of the basic rules of the game

After you've reached the level you are at in golf, you may focus on the present but forgetting the fundamentals of golf (considering these as being learned). But, if you'd like to have the best possible strike with the ball, it's not too bad to return towards the start. One way you can get an appropriate amount of golf ball the correct way is to increase the effectiveness of your strike. It is essential to make sure that the point of impact is located in the middle of the face and, in addition, you need be aware of your downswing, making sure to maintain that the club is in the correct position. club.

It is important to be aware that golf is not founded on the notion of taking the ball off the ground. It is a sport that requires precision and precision; the player must use the entire body to move to the optimal position. The player is also positioned the club so where the club actually gathers the ball before the low point is achieved. The speed of the swing can be a factor in equal measure, which ensures an excellent final.

Leaning forward is more important than you imagine

If you'd like to have an expert level of contact with your golf ball, you must consider forward leaning with the respect it merits. Begin by practicing your game using the forward lean, and then figuring out how simple it is to raise the ball into the air. If you're successful then you can progress to larger swings, until you are able to take a full swing.

The forward lean may appear like a daunting task to master, but the more you do it, the easier it becomes. Be sure that the weight you are putting on is toward the side leaning by letting your body rotate to the right position (as as mentioned earlier, this is the best way to ensure the most effective shot). Also don't put too much importance on your posture or posture, because you'll lose the desire to enjoy yourself and which means you'll miss out on the chance to create some fantastic shots.

Tees is a reliable companion

You probably already know that the tee is only allowed for the first shot on every hole.

However, you shouldn't ignore it and make use of it as often as you're allowed to and even on your practice course. Tees can assist you in making some great shots, and help you improve your confidence in all aspects of your game.

Tee gate drill

The tee gate exercise can assist you in determining whether there is a problem to your swing direction or not. What you should do is grab two tees, putting one of them at a distance of one inch from the club head, and on the heel's side and the other in the same space as the head of the club, however, on the opposite right side. Practice your short game on the tees and try to spot your tendency (too inwards or outwards). When you have identified an issue you can address it, and improve your swing.

Food to think about

1.) Are there other factors that could assist you in improving the overall contact you have with the ball on golf?

2.) Does it make sense to cause a mistake in your forward lean? If so then how?

3.) Is the ball's weight able to affect how close the contact point is (with the ball)? If the answer is yes what is the reason?

Chapter 10: Training For Golf: Mental Strength

Anonymous "In golf as with all things, it's the execution that really makes an impact."

For a long time, golfers were keen on enhancing their skills to play this unique game. Today things have changed significantly and it's no surprise that the passions of golfers are not just based on their golf skills but other factors too. One example is that one of the primary factors to be perfected is the golf swingwith which is largely ignored the other elements. However, this has resulted in a shift in the mental outlook of the majority of golfers (lack of mental physical toughness).

If you're looking to enhance your mental concentration The most crucial thing is to train at the most difficult level. Don't practice the things you're already familiar with. Instead try to put yourself in different situations. Through experiencing new experiences including the practice facility and also at the practice range, you can discover some new facts about yourself, particularly as far as your strength and weakness are in question. If you can succeed at these things then you'll also be able achieve your full potential on your golf courses.

Mental toughness is a key component

There are many elements that support the notion of mental toughness. As you'll have the chance to study in the subsequent paragraphs. If you are able to work at these components, with perseverance and patience and perseverance, you'll be able to achieve the level you desire of mental toughness.

The first thing you must keep in mind is the strength. Although strength is something is often demonstrated by golfers but it is more important when used at the right time. It is important to demonstrate your that you are strong when you're in a difficult situation or in a stressful one learning to become at ease regardless of the situation. This kind of courage will allow you to rise above any circumstance, particularly when confronted with tough competition. Never be afraid to take on pressure, regardless of how challenging it might be. Be sure to act as if every shot counts in the same way, because, as you can imagine... that really is.

Flexibility is the next aspect to be considered, but not in the manner you may imagine. It's not about your body's flexibility however this is crucial as it gets. Instead, we're discussing the ability to adjust to a range of situations, without affecting your performance. A lot of players succeed only when their requirements are met. When they are placed on a different course , or in situations where they must play in different conditions their results are nowhere to be seen.

Flexibleness and creativity are inextricably linked and help to accept things as they are, and while at the same time being able to adjust to any situation. The ability to think with a flexible mind can mean the difference between surviving stress and failure. It also allows you to remain open to new ideas and engage your creativity to the highest degree. To increase your ability to adapt, what you need to do is to take different clubs and go to the practice area, in different weather conditions. Try different types of shots, and make sure you go out regardless of the weather or other circumstances. The concept is to step outside from your comfortable zone that will make you less rigid and consequently, more flexible.

Maintaining a balance is something that you must keep in mind at all times regardless of whether you're in a match or playing on the range. Be sure to stay focused on every shot. being balanced means you don't become too excited, or, in the opposite or too easily disengaged. Mental balance is something is something you should be working on as as, if not even more than any other aspect that affects your golf performance and ability.

Be aware of your thoughts and don't be afraid to cut out thoughts negative ones or, perhaps negative. If you're struggling to concentrate on your thoughts, it could be that you are overthinking. This is the most significant issue. Try a simple exercise to boost your mental concentration. What you should be able to do is count how many negative or negative thoughts you've had over just a few hours. As your next move, attempt to get rid of them, each one at a time until you get to the goal of having zero (no negative or discouragement thoughts, but more of a positive attitude).

The word stamina is commonly utilized in relation to golf in reference to the extent to which a player is able to withstand the rigors of playing a golf round (or even). But when it comes to mental strength the notion of stamina acquires a totally new significance. It is the ability to conserve mental energy regardless of how demanding or emotional the game of golf could turn out to be. The players who show mental strength are also those who adhere to their strategy of the game, and not letting other players or the conditions on the course impact their performance.

Myths concerning mental toughness

In the realm of mental toughness and golf training There are a lot of myths you must know about. For instance, it is commonly believed that mental toughness is something that can't be learnedsince it is a natural ability. However, this isn't the case particularly since there are a myriad of methods and strategies you could employ in order to improve your mental concentration.

In the same way there is a misperception about golfers with mental toughness. A lot of people view them as a bit cocky and unfriendly this, however is not in line with how things work in actual reality. The last, but certainly not least another myth is that mental strength is only used when you're a winner at golf; it's not just a myth however the best way to use mental toughness is utilized when you're in a tough situation and are faced with a tough competition or in poor conditions.

Simple tips to keep your mental strength

* Distinguish you as a person from your role as a golfer - this helps you conserve all of your energy to allow you to play the correct method, no matter what conditions or competitions at the course.

Be aware of your body language. It is claimed that 90% of communication happens non-verbally, the body language of a person playing a crucial role in this regard. Be aware of your body language as it will reveal details about your mental state. When you're stressed out cortisol levels are rising and it is evident on the whole body. However when you're calm cortisol levels are lower and you are able to concentrate on your sport.

Positive thinking - train yourself to think positively even when you believe there's no rationale behind it. A positive attitude can trick the brain , and thus aid in getting out of difficult situations. If you behave as if that you're doing well then you'll also achieve your desired goals. Remember to pay attention towards your body language as you can, displaying confidence through all your pores. This will assist you in dealing stress in a more efficient way and, in the same time it will guarantee that you perform better under stress.

Food to think about

1.) What is mental strength in the context of your personal words?

2.) What other aspects do you think are associated with mental toughness (in golfers)?

3.) Do you believe that mental strength will be all you can do to aid you in dealing with stress when you're playing golf?

Chapter 11: Putting Stroke: Expert Level

Arnold Palmer: "Putting is like wisdom, it is natural talent, and partly the accumulation of knowledge."

From the time you begin to play golf, you're taught that the stroke of putting is an essential aspect to the sport. It's tempting to believe that it's easy to master, but it really requires a lot of effort to master this particular element. Additionally, it is difficult to master the putting stroke to an expert stage, particularly when you try to do the whole thing by yourself, with no any help from an expert. We've gathered a variety of relevant facts to assist in improving your putting skills and eliminate any issues you experience when you're trying to learn.

How do you prepare for the stroke of putting

The most crucial thing you need to keep in mind is that the stroke you use to put is usually negatively affected by rigidity. When you put, you need to manage your muscles, but that doesn't necessarily mean you have to show excessive rigidity. The stroke of putting requires sensitivity as well as the ability to take a decision directly right there, and with great vision. Of course, it is impossible to achieve the perfect putting stroke without considering the stroke's mechanics. Regarding your thoughts be sure not to let them interfere with your stroke and you'll not be able to make the shot you want.

Many players even those who have reached an expert level believe that the performance in putting is purely dependent on one's ability to perform mechanically. Although mechanics are a part of the equation however they aren't the only factors to consider (as previously mentioned). If you are spending too much of your time looking at grip putter, stance, swing, you'll forget about the larger overall picture. Instead of focusing solely on mechanics it may be more beneficial to focus more on the control of your muscles.

The motor control system is the pillar of putting that is a skill that requires a lot of practice, and is something only a handful of players actually realize. It is not only a mechanical move the putting stroke demands an ideal harmony between mind and body. It's a difficult ability, starting with mechanics, and ending with mental awarenessthat is essential to ensure the proper control.

It is clear that golf is a sport that requires both fine and gross motor skills is simple to grasp, particularly since golf is a sport that requires the involvement of all body parts throughout the game. Every muscle contraction is crucial along with anticipating the future while keeping the mind always in control. This means that motor control is not possible without the mental capacity to plan and make decisions. The brain is the one that determines every move as well as controlling our bodies so that we can achieve the goals we want to achieve.

Essential elements of the stroke for putting

There are many essential elements that are crucial to the success of a putting stroke in order to excel in this area of golf, you'll need to improve on each of them (in the same way). Therefore, putting requires the following skills: vision (you utilize it to collect details about direction, distance and other elements like rain or wind) and imagery (you need to be able to visualize yourself having a good shot, since this can put you on the right path) Attention (your mind should be focused solely on that putt, with your mind not wandering off unnecessarily) and control by mechanical means (mechanics remain vital to the success of a putt).

How to proceed

If you've attained an expert level it doesn't mean that you must not be paying attention to the actions of the stroke. These are still as vital in helping you to succeed regardless of tension or pressure you're experiencing. The first step is to ensure to make an instant analysis of the speed you want to achieve and the course, in addition to of other variables that could affect the stroke (weather conditions, for instance). Next, you develop an outline of your exact stroke (planning). Thirdly, you pay focus on the motor control and mechanics while making sure you are prepared to perform the stroke. The last, but certainly not least, by utilizing all the above components and you are able to create the stroke successfully.

Drills to improve your level of proficiency

Everyone is aware of how effective drills can be regardless of what level you are currently. These drills can help you to develop your body and mind to be more effective in strokes. Therefore, prior to beginning your practice, the first thing you must do is grab the impact tape and put it to the surface of the putter's face.

The first drill is to make a selection of golf balls and set them in a two-by-two pattern in three different locations that is, 30to 20 to 10 feet (you are making six putts total). The aim in this practice is to roll the ball in a circle that is approximately 3 feet around the hole, also being referred to as "the safety zone. Repeat the same procedure for every distance before trying the drill from the opposite end of the hole (at three different distances, too).

The second exercise is to take twelve golf balls and this time, place them in an arc (three inches). Put them on a sloping portion of the green close to the hole (as previously mentioned). Then, try to move each ball around the circle, in an anticlockwise path (clockwise in case you're left-handed). It is crucial that your stance doesn't get dependent on the next ball that you're about to putt.

Once you're done, make certain to examine the impact tape so that you can see the quality of your made contact with. Don't be deceived in the event that you find numerous marks as they indicate that you've worked to get better at what you do. Continue to practice and you'll see the impact area will decrease in a gradual manner but quite dramatically.

Food to think about

1.) What is the reason you believe excessive stiffness can have such negative effects on the stroke of putting?

2.) Do stroke mechanics and motor control have more importance?

3.) How much does your mental awareness affect the performance of the putt?

Chapter 12: How Can A Golf Teacher Assist You In Your Professional Level?

Anonymous "An exceptional instructor will be difficult to come across, difficult to part with , and difficult for one to lose."

If you are a novice to the golf world instructors can be an invaluable resource. They can guide you through the basics of golf as well as the equipment and methods that can be employed. Additionally, they can provide valuable advice on how you can grow as a golfer and enhance your current skills or capabilities. As you begin to improve and progress to the next level you may not accept the need for an instructor. This chapter will show, an instructor can be beneficial, no matter the stage at which you are.

Whatever your stage, you'll want to find a coach who will help you achieve your full potential. You must realize that such a commitment is vital, particularly in order to increase your skills and be the best you can be. The choice of an instructor is an issue of compatibility since you must ensure that both of you have a similar mindset. The instructor must be able to understand your requirements and needs, as well as employ modern techniques of communication and give you instant feedback about your skills and capabilities in golf. A golf instructor who does not engage in constant contact isn't one you'd like to be on your side.

When choosing an instructor who can assist you at an expert level, there are variety of factors to consider. The first and most important thing is that you should ensure that the instructor you choose has a good reputation and has the required qualifications. Then, you should be aware of the costs that are demanded for the services offered. The location is also important since you don't wish to travel hundreds of miles to meet together with your trainer. Like we said earlier it is best to stay away from instructors who don't believe in using modern technology or methods of communication.

The assistance that instructors can provide at this stage has a lot to be attributed to skill. You have grasped the basics of the game together with the equipment and strategies which can be employed. You've also learned the most advanced methods learning how to decrease your score, increase your putting skills and many other components. The coach will conduct an evaluation of your current performance while taking the time to learn about your personality.

There is a very important concern you need to consider is whether your golf instructor has the necessary training and knowledge to assist you in becoming an expert in golf? Find answers to that question by having an extended, but beneficial conversation with an expert. Ask about their golfing experience since many instructors have had a long and prosperous career. They are now sharing their expertise to anyone who are interested.

Talk about the method to teach and also the tools that are used to teach. For instance instructors can utilize swing aids, regardless of their level. Instructors should have strong justifications for using them specifically in advanced or expert levels. Be sure to ask questions about the tools employed in teaching like videos and ball flight monitors, fitting of clubs and swing path tracing equipment (these show the direction of swing from three different angles). Be sure to inquire about feedback, communication and contact, since these are crucial aspects to think about.

A different aspect that is interesting is that an instructor could introduce you to a group of experts. Every expert belonging to this group can assist you in improving the overall quality of your performance. The experts you'll come into contact with are fitness instructors psychologists, fitness instructors (trained specifically for and working with golfers) and nutritionists, travel managers educators, club fitters as well as physical therapy. Ask the instructor questions about the team, and make certain to mention other experts that could be beneficial to you.

Many golfers, once getting to the level of expert, want to go pro. If you share a similar desire, you should look for a teacher with experience in this area as well (competitive experience). It's a source of confidence knowing that your instructor went through the same procedure and has worked hard to beat existing competition and reach the goals he or she wants to achieve. At the end of the day, it is about developing common communication lines and sharing experiences that assist you in growing. Furthermore, knowing that other people have been there at the same level, you'll have a better chance of getting through any difficulties that may occur along the road.

It is also crucial that the teacher can communicate on your level to ensure that you comprehend everything on the first go around and do not have to ask questions constantly. In this case the instructor must be able to instruct you the way he considers appropriate to your particular situation, and not just what worked for them as a player. In the end, the primary goal of the instructor's help is help you reach your full potential, not to imitate the success of other players. This is why you are free to ask your instructor any type of question and also require demonstration of various abilities.

Trust is possibly an crucial factors to be considered in working alongside an educator. If you aren't confident in him or her and the reverse is to the other, the odds of success are extremely low. However it may take time before you start to trust your coach and their innate abilities. The most important thing is that you get to an agreement of confidence, so that your instructor is able to assist you in helping enhance every aspect of your game.

The best thing when having an instructor on your side is the fact that the instruction is one-on-one. Private lessons are private and give you the chance to work on every aspect that makes up the sport, regardless of whether we're talking about shorter games, swing, or the putt. Additionally, you will have access to cutting-edge golf technology, like the analysis of your swing and ball flight radars in addition to balance plates, ultrasound and putt systems. A few instructors also utilize educational tools to assist you comprehend the way certain theories work in the golf world (for instance how to swing).

It is likely that the instructor may resort to the analysis of video swings using computers, to assess the needs of your students for teaching, instruction and improvement. Based on the findings of the analysis video, the instructor will create a custom teaching program that can serve as the basis for the change. In some cases, the program could include instruction on swing technique and course management, or putt. What is most important is to develop into an expert in playing golf, and taking you to the next step in your game.

Food to think about

1.) Give three examples of ways that an instructor could be beneficial at the expert level.

2.) What should you look for in an instructor? characteristics you should be looking to find from an instructor?

3.) What makes instructors with a competitive background better suited to these kinds of teaching experience?

Chapter 13: Practice Drills

Bobby Jones: "You swing your best when you've got only a few items to contemplate."

In the context of golf, people tend to throw around the term "talent" around as if it were something that magically can make you better, but not exceptional, at playing this sport. It's actually not enough, or even at a minimum, to be able to compete with your native capabilities. You perform at the best when you train frequently and engaging in various situations , and working to improve your weaknesses and strengths.

Training exercises, no matter the level you may reach, will provide a tremendous benefit. They aid in identifying the potential weaknesses and strengths. However they push you out of your comfortable zone, which can lead to that you can reduce your handicap and overall score. In the following paragraphs there are various drills to practice which are certainly worthy of your attention (even even if you're at an advanced level, you can gain a lot by trying them out).

1. Training drill Full swing

The process of improving your swing is among the most difficult things to do and even at a professional level, you may encounter some difficulties. First, you must get rid of any other issues You can't expect to be able to take a full swing when you're focused on your family, work or any other things that require your attention.

To master this drill, it is suggested to make a practice swing prior to each shot you're about to hit. Be patient and clear your mind. practicing the best technique for both the practice swing as well as actually hitting. The idea behind this is the fact that the exercise swing serves as a kind of practice that helps you to work on fundamental elements like the backswing. When you've completed the perfect practice swing you will find it extremely easy to hit that actual shot. Make use of this drill to remain focussed on the key elements of the swing, which includes the impact point and your contact quality.

#2 Practice drill: dead aim

This drill is a chance to practice and make sure you to put your mental abilities to use. Take a walk to your practice green (tee) and imagine your most favorite course (alternatively an option which you're acquainted with). In your head, you'll go through all nine or 18 holes, minus the putts. Make use of your clubs in the right way for each shot, observing your practice routine (mentally).

By using this exercise, you'll improve your mental imagery as well as, simultaneously you'll be engaged in a different type of exercise. You could even enjoy a some fun and make this exercise into a game. all you need to do is give the points you earn. For instance you should award a point awarded for a shot that is in line with your expectations and no points should be given for shots that are not acceptable. However when you hit poor shots, that is a loss of one point. Poor shots can include tops and chunks, so be sure you consider all of them into consideration. The goal is to ensure to improve your overall goals.

#3 Practice drill: chipping

In this particular exercise you must practice on the green and take five golf balls. Create a target hole, and then try to hit chips. Choose various lengths to practicing. The primary goal of this exercise is to hit each of five balls in a short distance as long as is feasible (within the length of the club in the hole). If you don't have enough knowledge of the area, you may be able to increase your distance (two and three clubs).

If you are able to hit the balls within that distance, you can boost your difficulty in the exercise. This time, you'll have to smash balls inside the steel club. It may seem challenging, even if it's not at first however, with persistence and practice you'll definitely be able to achieve great accomplishment.

#4 Practice drill: five-foot putt

As the name suggests, this practice demands that you spend longer on the practice field and practicing how to putt five feet. The goal is to continue making those putts until you have reached fifty consecutive shots. If you've missed the one ball of golf, then you will need return to the beginning. This could require a lot of energy and time, but ultimately it will all be worth it. Additionally, when you reach fifty and fifty, you'll surely experience extreme levels of pressure that can be used as a great way to prepare for the future competitions.

By practicing this drill it is possible to enhance your game short and test how you can play under stress. Most important is to not stop and continue to work until you have reached your goal. If you think it's too excessive, stop by stretching your spine. Return to the green where you practice and continue.

#5 Practice drill: hitting wedges

From the moment you play golf your first time you're educated that wedges can be utilized to hit short-range shots and pitching. If you're a beginner or have reached an professional level, using wedges is still equally crucial. To practice this drill you can test hitting wedges, but not at full speed, but more or less than half of the distance you planned to use initially.

What you need to do is choose three different distances and attempt hitting ten ball at each hole you want to target. Again, you could make this exercise into a game by awarding you a point for every ball that gets within the holes (you will need to be aware of how far). Always strive to beat your score until you're happy with the score you've accomplished (of obviously, your best score is 30).

#6 Practice drill: sand

Sand shots aren't easy to master, no matter the amount of experience you have acquired in the field. This is why this drill is more than a must to test. In the first place, it is suggested, as with other drills, that you clear your mind of any other thoughts. Clear mind can aid in making better shots.

What you need to select is a space you can practice in, but always within an opening. You can pick the radial distancebased on your capabilities and previous experiences, but generally it will range between 10 and 50 feet. Five golf balls are taken and attempt to put them in the hole you want to hit, or as close as much as is feasible. You can award yourself points for success shots. You can improve the level of difficulty by reducing the space you work on.

Food to think about

1.) Why are drills for practice so crucial even at the professional level?

2.) When should people engage in exercises for practice, to your opinion?

3.) What can an uncluttered mind help you succeed, using terms of what you say?

Chapter 14: Tours For Golfers Of The Expert Level: And Tournaments

Larry Nelson: "There's not any stress on the golf circuit. The first tee walk is not similar to walking through jungle of the field of battle."

If a golfer reaches the level of expert golf, it's likely that they will also show the desire to participate in pro golf tournaments. They are held on a regular basis and are under the watchful oversight of PGA or similar organizations. To participate at the events held within these tour, players need to be a member of. Certain golf events and golf tours are restricted only to the elite and displaying an impressive level of competitiveness (hence the reason that some athletes may not get to participate in these tournaments).

The PGA Tour is, without doubt, among the most well-known professional golf tours around the globe attracting players with a great reputation and long-term career prospects. It is followed by the European Tour follows, being well-known all over the world for its highly prestigious tournaments and lucrative prizes. It is interesting to note that there are tournaments and tours which are specifically reserved for players who are senior (men older than 50). At these events, you will see many famous athletes who demonstrate their professional-level abilities and talents in the numerous tournaments that are held. Women are welcome to take part in tournaments and tours that are specially designed for women in different countries around the globe.

The most prestigious golf tournaments are held under the umbrella name"men's major championships" or "men's big championships" and include: PGA Championship, The Masters, The Open Championship and The US Open. Women's major championships, too however, they could comprise any number of tournaments (without any specific calendar of events that was previously agreed upon). Some of the most prestigious golf tournaments devoted to female golfers they include: The Evian Championship, ANA Inspiration, US Women's Open, Women's British Open and Women's PGA Championship. They're usually organized in conjunction with the LPGA Tour.

Based on what was said in the previous paragraphs, you've probably been able to see that the main goal of a professional tour is to give players access to tournaments in golf, along with their schedules and geographical place being made available to interested (and qualified) players.

It is crucial to realize that it isn't easy and, in some cases, impossible to earn a decent living from tournaments and golf tournaments. This is due to the fact that there aren't many golfers who can succeed all the time but, being a participant to tournaments and golf requires that participants pay entry fees in addition to expenses for travel and lodging. In most cases, it is required to hire an assistant, which requires that there is an additional amount to consider.

The pressure of golf tournaments can rise to unbelievable levels, particularly since there are specific rules that are designed to limit the number of participants after an additional round. When deciding who goes on to the next two rounds scores average (so so far) is considered. So, the top players are chosen for the final round which means that the amount of competitiveness (and that's why the stress) is raised. It is obvious that only a limited amount of golfers are likely to take home the trophy or win the event that is being played, therefore it is difficult to invest in an event and not come back with a dime.

As was stated above, you are not able to play in golf tournaments and tours when you're not an active member. The one exception to this rule is for players with exceptional skills, who are permitted to play as non-members. If they want to take part on this tour, they must be able to demonstrate their accomplishments to be eligible for a tour card. However, they may not be able to participate in every event that is scheduled in the course (some such events may be reserved for the most elite players or those with a history of winning other well-known tournaments or tours).

What is the process for becoming an official member of a golf tour? In general, those who have demonstrated the ability to win an entry tournament or tournament, may be invited to join more reputable tour (entry tournaments are generally referred to in the context of qualifying courses). If an individual has shown the highest level of achievement on a golf course in competitions as a non-member, they may be asked to compete as an official member. There is a possibility that golfers who have had success in other events can be invited to join at a top event or tour, but it isn't always the scenario.

From a practical point viewpoint, it's important to pointed out that there are some clear distinctions between the major golf courses as well as those less well-known. They allow professional golfers to join the tour after paying the fee for entry (no other requirements). Another major difference is the financial rewards given to each golf tour specifically. From a financial point of view the tour that offers the most appealing rewards can be described as The PGA Tour, the European Tour and the LPGA Tour.

Food to think about

1.) Your opinion on what is the reason you believe that men and women's championships are arranged in a different way?

2.) How do you feel of the special tournaments and tours that are geared towards senior players?

3.) Are there any other motives to consider why it is difficult to earn a decent living solely from a participation in golf tournaments and golf tours?

Chapter 15: Water Golf Is An Unforgettable Experience

Anonymoussays "Life can be more enjoyable when playing golf."

If you enjoy spending your time on the range for driving, you may be interested in visiting an underwater golf precision range. It's a unique experience, as well as a challenging experience that is suitable for an experienced golfer.

A driving range like this is usually situated over a stunning lake or pond, and has floating greens that offer the opportunity to test your skills for the rest of your life. By practicing on these professionally-designed areas, you are able to test not only your swinging distance but also the level of accuracy. The greens floating are set at various distances, and are accessible to golfers with different levels of expertise. Some are equipped with artificial mats, whereas others are made of natural grass.

You can also train on sand bunkers putt greens, and other water dangers.

When you read about water golf it's normal to wonder if it's a safe activity or not. Each water-based green, or hit area is constructed to give you the safety you require. Some are enclosed, and a majority contain netting that is protected. The hitting bays with roofs are more appealing, since they protect against weather elements as well as preventing the launching of golf balls that are not in the area of swinging. Because of the protective roof you can practise your swings even if it's sunny outside or it is raining.

If the range is one you're going to, it's likely that the hitting area has cement placed on top of mats. This allows the golf balls to roll easily into the water, and decreases the chance from golf balls getting picked up by others. Additionally the hitting bays as well as floating greens are constructed so that they offer a lesser chance of injury.

If you're feeling like the driving range is becoming boring, then you must go to the accuracy of the water golf range. The majority the ranges in gorgeous areas, offering breathtaking views of hills or mountains. As was mentioned earlier that the spaces that are available for training are referred to as floating greens or hitting bays which are either covered or covered. For the flooring, it could be synthetic or top-quality grass, based on the area. Certain ranges offer additional practice areas, which include pitching, chipping, and putting.

There is nothing better than hitting golf balls on an idyllic lake? Try this out at least once to see the excitement this type of practice is. There is the possibility to try hitting these targets in the lake, or, should you wish to, you can try to the hole-in one directly on the green that is floating. Not to be left out you can take advantage to hit the floating buoys that are have been marked for use in practice (yardage in terms of yards).

There is no reason to think that the green course at your range isn't worth your time. However, if you're that you need to change things up and trying something different water sports, then aquatic golf must be at the top of your list of things to do. There is the possibility to hit floating golf balls and most of them in stunning scenery, on an amazing pond or lake. Because of the innovative layout of the range, it won't be like there is a limit on space or anything similar to that. Additionally, you'll have the chance to observe how floating golf balls actually quite similar to regular ones, due to the most modern advancements in technology used to manufacture them.

Another reason, and it is vital, one for that you should think about water golf. If you're used to participating in tours and tournaments, then you are aware of how difficult it may be to stay ahead of the other players. Because of this, playing golf in the water could give you an advantage over others who are on the same level.

Therefore, it's not just an exciting way to test it out, but at the moment, it gives you an opportunity to stand in the crowd.

Accuracy range of the golf course in the water Practical information

The floating or hitting bays greens may have different dimensions, based on the distance and demands of players. There are smaller floating holes that are commonly utilized in lakes (where huge islands might have been difficult or impossible to put in). They are small in diameter, but they give you the chance to test your swinging distance as well as accuracy.

Then, at the next level are floating greens that are, naturally, larger in dimension. They are available in a variety of designs, like circles or oval, which are incorporated with the other range of design (kidney-shaped greens for target practice can also be found). These greens give players of various levels the opportunity to improve the swing distance as well as accuracy. It is an interesting fact that in several ranges, the top of the surface is UV-resistant for greater protection.

Not to be left out is the island greens. They have an enormous size and are commonly found on lakes. They are made of artificial lawn or genuine grass giving players with the thrilling experience of water golf. The range could include artificial vegetation as well as various hazards, like bunkers made of sand.

Food to think about

1.) What are the reasons why aqua golf is thrilling?

2.) Do you think hitting golf balls across lakes or ponds is more difficult than the normal exercise at the range?

3.) Could this be going to be the new driving ranges ? water golf?

Chapter 16: Golf Technology For Professional-Level Players

Tiger Woods: "It's cool today to play golf."

In a world that is dominated by cool gadgets and technology it is not a surprise to find numerous technological advances that golfers can benefit from. They can be beneficial for players of every level including experts and can help them enhance or track their performance. Continue reading to discover new golf technologies that you must explore.

Smart shoes

In the world of smart watches and similar wearable technologies it was just one step. The smart shoes can provide feedback about your swing, based on the information collected during these movements. The data is gathered through sensors for pressure, which are located in their soles. The information is transferred to your smartphone by using the Bluetooth technology.

Based on the information you gather it is possible to analyze your golf swing, and contrast it against similar swings of professional golfers (these can be found in the library of swings that is included with the program). You can not only analyze your swing in comparison to those of pros, but you are also able to send the information you have gathered to your golf instructor (he/she could provide their own feedback based upon the data you send).

From a practical the view of practicality, you need to be aware that the best shoes can be found in a classic or sport style. The midsoles are light to ensure comfort. The interior lining gives the skin improved breathability, while the outsole's grip ensures best performance on the course. In terms of battery life generally, it's approximately five days.

Golf app for putt (with sensors that snap on)

There are a lot of applications that are dedicated to golf, this particular app is more intriguing. This is due to the fact that it evaluates your putting stroke at as you execute the stroke (real-time feedback). Additionally, it provides the ability to access interactive exercises as well as also an array of instructional materials (information that comes from PGA instructors who are professionals).

The sensor that snaps on is the most intriguing aspect of this new technology, since it can be connected to any type of putter. It collects information about the stroke you are using and also give feedback on the movements the body is going through. The stroke you are analyzing is evaluated from multiple angles. You can look back at your stroke because of the video playback feature integrated (the information is synchronized to the data collected by the snap-on sensor). Furthermore, the information you input is stored and saved in cloud storage, which allows for accessibility to your information. The application can be used to both outdoor and indoor practice of putting strokes.

Oversized putter grip

If you're still experiencing difficulties with your grip you might consider trying the putter grip that is oversized to try. Due to the unique shape, this can limit the movement of the muscles that are small in wrists (and implicitly, hands). It will also allow for larger muscles to participate when putting. shoulders, back and arm muscles, increasing the accuracy and consistency.

The gimmick of the large grip for the putter is provided by the weight of 50 grams added in the grip's butt. Incredibly, there are two additional options that are available, namely that the 25 grams and the 75 grams of weight. You can see that the best part is that you are able to alter the weight according to your preferences and your actual performance.

Rangefinder

In terms of wearable technology the rangefinder is a piece that you can't live without. The first thing you should know is that you must be aware that it's incredibly light, and sleek in its style and. Its biggest benefit is that it provides details from over 30000 courses. It also provides information on driving distance and greens as well as yardage and swinging accuracy for the holes.

There are two additional motives to take a look at this innovative idea. Oneis that it provides excellent visibility regardless of the time of day or the weather outside. The second is that it comes with an exclusive design, based in the principles behind ergonomics to ensure that it doesn't interfere with how you play in any manner. In addition, it comes with a finger-friendly tap sensor, and you've got the ideal technology for you to test in the field of golf.

Golf simulator

For someone who has experience in the golf world It is almost impossible to not have heard of golf simulators. They allow you to play playing golf to an entirely different level and having fun simultaneously.

Modern golf simulators can provide challenging experiences in that they include live play, which is an additional option (for playing the shorter game). In addition, when you use the golf simulator, players are offered the opportunity to learn golf on famous golf courses. For instance, imagine getting a hole-in one on the course of golf on Pebble Beach or making the perfect shot on the green at St. Andrews. You can practice chipping and putting, pitching or putting, it's all yours to decide and it is certain that you will be having the most enjoyable time that you'll ever remember. This is an engaging experience that can aid in improving your overall performance and improve your points of strengths as well as weaknesses.

Food to think about

1.) Are there other innovations in golf technology that merit a try?

2.) How will these new developments affect the game of golf?

3.) What do we have to look forward to from the future, in terms of golf's technological advancements (in your view)?

Chapter 17: Golf Tips

Golf is a game of free enterprise which is played with clubs as well as balls by those who are referred to as golfers. The balls are struck towards the golf holes on a course that requires players play as little as they can. Golf is the art of hitting the ball using a golf club starting from the tee.

The holes are equipped with tee boxes, where the game begins at the time of putting. The green is where the hole actually is. Golf is played on different playing surfaces. They are made up of roughs fairways, hazards, and roughs however, all of these fields are distinctive in their unique arrangement and layouts. You will be amazed that golf unlike other ball games is not a requirement for an identical field. Golf is played with a course or surface which is laid out in a progression which has nine or eighteen holes. In a golf game the goal is to score the least strokes a player can hit. This type of play is referred to as the stoke play. In a match play one golfer has the lowest score on several holes, and thus becomes the winner. Of the two distinct forms of play that stroke play is regarded to be the more popular, even though the rules vary.

A team can be made up of two or one players. Single is when one player competes against another player, while a foursome happens when two players are playing against each other. Threesomes are where one player is playing against two players, playing a ball between the two. The game is played with each team playing a ball off an edging ground into a hole using successive strokes.

Strategies for Golf that Make an Amateur into a Pro

They have developed their swing speed and make fairways more open with regularity that is military. Professionals increase their ball strike as well as iron game. To enhance their skills, they find their way out of bunker-like magicians. Through a variety of styles, they are able to strike unique flop shots from forty yards from. When they master their method, a high level of control is demonstrated and at the right pace, becoming the best golfers they are. They're masters at fixing it using all the power of their bodies to win amazing wins. An examination of their swing shows that they have teachers who put their brains before their muscles to create unforgettable stingers. Therefore, the importance professionalism in golf can't be denied.

The amateur has to set the goal of advancing from a 20 handicap down to 12 handicap. The reality is that few amateurs have taken on the details of transforming into world-class golfers, and thus their game has been an unintentional affair on the course. In essence, amateur golfers do not have the time to warm up properly, and they employ traditional courses management. Their style of play is based to be aggressive, while they're required to be cautious. This is shown by focusing on the equipment, not the approach to technicality and the instructions regarding the game, but the good news is that there is the potential for substantial improvement in the pertinent information. This guide will give you the chance to rethink how to get the professional you've always wanted when you were an amateur.

PRACTICAL GOLF Skills

It is a good idea to warm up Chipping and Pitching

One difference between amateurs and professional golfer is how they warm up. The amateur will pull his drivers out of the bag and then immediately begin playing once he is to the course. Professionals will however, use the short iron wedge, which might be an eighth or nine. Just like the recipe, he'll proceed by using half or quarter-sized swings and settle with great concentration. The club head is vital and the professional will sense it circling around his palm. With his basic technique, he creates an easy rhythm that permits an unforced swing. The eye of the professional are not focused on the distance the ball covers, but rather the impact he makes when striking it. He'll hit ten or eight powerful pitches and extend his backswing, which is then transformed into an entire swing. The process will continue as the professional hits powerful short irons. He will then slowly gaining 7 irons, while combining half swings, and then moving into full swings with an iron that is long and woods. If an amateur is able to take this suggestion then he's already getting close to the highest level. It is basically an approach to goal which involves the stimulation of muscles. In a steady slow, steady rhythm, and lastly, the necessary touch with the ball will help players improve their game. It is now possible to move onto the starting tee in confidence. Three steps to pitch your ball in the correct direction each time.

Training Golf Skills by setting a schedule

When practicing the golf game the routine allows one to gauge their improvement in his mastery of the game. For instance, hitting 10 golf shots during practice is a good way to start with your goal when you begin your journey to becoming an expert golfer. Set a goal of seventy percent for short putts or 3 to twelve feet, which equals one to four meters. For iron shots, set an aim of seventy per cent or greater, and apply similar rules to wood shots. Try a seventy percent wedge technique within one hundred yards or the equivalent of ninety meters. This should be the minimum for any player to become more proficient. The following are suggestions and techniques that have been tested and can turn amateurs to professional. This can greatly enhance one's performance should he be willing to spend a bit of time, effort, and effort about the game.

Create a strong pre-shot procedure

Take a look at the pre-shot process of two professional shooters You will see it's the same. They do the same thing and the variation between one shot and the next isn't more than two minutes. The routine might appear superficial, but it's the method he has created. Anyone who wants to make it to the professional level should adapt their own approach which in turn will become his home. Take a break from the massive number .Just like with humans, keeping away from risk being an amateur is a must. The risk increases when the choice is the possibility of a double or even the triple bogey. Refraining from blowing holes is an essential and reliable method of reducing the handicap of amateurs. After you've learned this skill, you will be able to improve your game. Improve the most crucial shot in golf is to sink putts. are a vital aspect for a golfer looking to become a discerning practice. It starts by making three or four putts. If you are able to do this consistently, your scores will drop and confidence in making longer putts is born. The only way to improving your putting is with plenty of practice. Golf is a game of perseverance, you should develop the habit of sinking a few putts every week. Join with the best players. They are engaging, and those who have been through prior to you, are just as proficient like the sport itself. Learn more about better players and play a round in golf. If you have a ten-year-old, playing with a twenty-something might not be the most profitable. Knowing the times when tournaments are scheduled and giving them a go is a method of assessing the level of your game. The mystery surrounding amateurs is the fact that they go off with force on the tee, only to fade off when it comes time in decisive strokes. The tragedy is that they are thrown into the bunker that is big in the event of tough chipping and difficult putts. They fail to overcome it and lose. The most important thing to remember in golf is to dedicate yourself to each shot and not focusing on the goals and projections when you make the shots. This is a fundamental principle that every amateur should adhere to. A single shot at a. Keep your focus on the present moment and leave out the results of your scores and the results of the final round up to the final.

You must also remember that golf is one that is enjoyable. The process before you hit the ball is a guideline which will help you stay in the right place throughout every shot. It's not easy because your mind is tangled between the outcome and the task in front of you. It is in the best interest of the player to put the thoughts of wandering to the back of their mind.

Make a Safety Plan

A game that is short is just a nugget during the game of golf. The best way to approach it is to make the illusion of security. It's an opportunity to save you from you are faced with the shove. It could be a choice from the utility clubs. It could also be aiming at on the rough to your left. This could lead to the reduction in your grip, and then you might strike a cut. This is your weapon of choice an security device that creates it possible for you to avoid the risk of racking a terrible number. Purchase equipment that is appropriate for your sport.

Right Equipment

The equipment is essential in winning a game of golf as the equipment is to winning. For those with high handicaps, it is recommended to purchase irons which improve their game as well as an exconerative driver. Mid handicappers should also utilize irons that can improve your game. It is crucial not to use an iron that is bigger than a five because it could hinder your game. The advancement of technology has allowed golfers to provide every golfer with an option to choose the best equipment that can make them winners. Golf clubs can be a difficult thing to play golf. Going to the golf club and purchasing a golf club isn't the best way to win, as a golf club has to be designed for the playing style of amateurs. Therefore, anyone who wants to become a professional needs to choose a club that is suitable. The length of is relative to the height of the person must be taken into consideration. A driver that is short for a player with a height that of six feet is the lowest point in his playing career. The weight of the driver be medium and the flexibility of its shaft must be adequate.

Create a game plan and stick to it

Prior to a tournament's start you should make the plan of action for how to get to every hole. It will help one not the wrong thing from his prior plans. A new strategy before the event could put you in disaster for the player with inconsistent executions and mistakes. It is possible to master the art of hitting a hybrid shot with three irons by making sure you are in the fairway before you are taking the shot. You can also hit a shorter and well-fixed iron on the front on the left side of green. The critical holes should be played backward. Create a few basic swing ideas. When you are in a calm and focused state one can make a decent swing. However, during the play session one's thoughts can be lost as one prepares to shoot. The solution to this is to cultivate a swing- idea and combining it with your routine for a short time to get the desired result. So that the downswing will not be impaired.

Visualize the shot

The idea of visualization is applicable to a game of golf. The ability to visualize the flight and character of the shot when it is landed on the green, or perhaps on the fairway can be very enriching. In the case of putting, the same approach should be followed. "You are the thing you think" can't be denied, in this instance. Take a lesson lessons. Golf lessons are an essential element in the development of an amateur to professional. Technology cannot alter the swing of a player who is less powerful. Thus, getting instruction on golf with professionals should be embedded to the golfer. It's not a gift with a freebie as there are fees however, the result is worth it when your game is improved significantly.

Use a Hammer Blow to generate more power

The speed in a swing can be achieved through the shoulders. The wrists are also sufficient when elbows are used. These crucial joints relax the same way as when someone is using the wooden hammer. The trick is to coordinate their movements , and consequently, great speed can be released. The concept is to develop the swing while you are standing on the other opposite side. From hand to elbow, one's right arm must be vertical. This is the ideal position for your swing.

THE DELIVERY

The upper right arm is positioned towards the side of your body with the hammer in the same position, swinging back into the body could force you to redirect the club to the outside and away and give you a powerful outside strike. It's as if you hit with a hammer. It's like hitting it upwards and downwards but not in a circle. Every swing must be synchronized by blending up and down. Professional golfers are typically prone to making numerous errors. One of the most common is the curve the ball takes when it's up in the air. It's the result of the player who plays the ball with an open or closed face. open face.

Tee the Ball

The one that takes the ball off the tee at a low angle is the preferred and efficient one. A lot of times the golfer might not find enough space on the lower side of the ball, and the shot that is skywards can end in a poor performance. The low tee appears as a sequel to the previous one, and thus makes it easier to follow and compare. The technique that takes the ball from the tee's low point is the most preferred and efficient option. Most of the time the golfer will not be able to get enough space in the lower portion of the ball, and the shot to the sky ends with a weak performance. The low tee is regarded as a follow-up to the previous one, and thus provides uniformity and is easy to follow and compare. The quality of the grip can not be understated since its use requires the use of both hands in a sync-

synchronized manner and gives the golfer an advantage. A two-V-grip is strengthened with the right hand when making your downwards swing. While gripped, many golfers do not allow their thumb to rest on the shaft due to the fear that it could break because of the pressure.

It is the Movement of Feet and Legs

The movements of legs and feet are vital. The shot that clears the ball from the tee at a low angle is the most preferred and efficient one. Most often the golfer might not find enough space on the lower side of the ball, and the shot that is skywards can end in a poor performance. The low tee is regarded as a continuation of the previous one which makes it uniform and it is easy to follow and compare.

Grip

The strength of the grip can't be understated since its use requires the use of both hands in a coordinated manner which gives the golfer an advantage. Two-V grips are strengthened using the left arm when making down swings. While gripped, many golfers don't allow their thumbs to rest on the shaft due to the fear that it could break because of pressure. You must learn to stand up while the feet are both flat and firmly on the ground. In order to balance the load, both legs must be equally distributing it. Then , they should have knees bent but not at an angle to be obvious. This is a position that is maintained the entire upward motion caused by the club. Next step lifting the leg's left heel, and begin pivoting it on the left foot. The arms then can be lifted up and down the club easily.

Upward and downward Swings

When swinging upwards the head of the club must be brought back in straight lines for a couple of inches, slowly brought back, but not too straight upwards (causing cutting) or too much in the traditional style. The speed of the swing is increased slowly. The elbows are held at a good angle, with the left wrist moving inwards and then finishing the upward swing just below the shaft. The body should not be allowed to swing. It must be able to pivot easily around the waist. The head must remain in a seated position. The weight is slowly shifted all over the right leg. As the left knee flexes and it rises as does the toe. There shouldn't be any jerks during the swing. When you swing downwards there must there be an increase in the speed, but not a movement whatsoever. The arms should remain in a straight line as the club descends with the elbows nearly touching the body. The right wrist shouldn't be allowed to climb up at the very top. The head remains motionless. Left hips are permitted to move slightly forward as the club comes down. The head is stationary. It is permitted to move up and down while the club is moving down. The right shoulder needs to be kept from falling too far. Following the impact the arms should allow the ball to move along as well as the body should move forward, with the latter move being carefully timed. The head can now be lifted. The arms should be positioned over the right hand above the left. Slices can be caused by being too close towards the ball pulling the arms in or falling onto the ball. It is generally caused by your head on the golf club being turned in a sloping manner when the ball is hit or by loosening the grip on the left hand in order to achieve satisfactory results. There is no doubt that playing a golf ball with a good technique is not something to be taught in just the span of a week or month. Help you with your bunker play little wonder that driving the golf ball correctly is something that should not be taught in a week or months. Help you with playing your golf bunker. If a golfer can to make his famous, wind-cheating stinger, and the world's most famous flop shot, or the smooth way that a professional can stripe a drive of 350 yards that cuts through the fairway aren't just accident and they aren't secrets either. It is true that practice when combined with talent have a significant impact on the playing golf. Professionals use different methods to apply the swing as well as their short-game skills. The result is that it comes to studying.

PHYSICAL fitness and diet

Golfers who combine their game with healthy food choices such as broccoli and chicken it reduces in body fat from 22 to 16 percent. The significance of fitness for golf is more than you think. Golf is a game that requires low intensity and is very sedentary. This makes it a game that can be considered a fitness activity as the swing requires the highest level of bodily fitness. It requires a lot of strength and getting your body ready to swing. The process of reducing the handicap is a serious business. From beginners to pros Golfers of all levels should be in top physical and mental fitness. Their backs strain constantly as hips continue to flex and require regular training. To prevent shoulder injuries that happen caused by playing golf, it is necessary to maintain regular fitness. This type of exercise should be integrated into your weekly exercise routine. This workout will work the quads (muscle of the thigh which can extend the legs) as well as your glutes. This exercise should be repeated with the other hand. Repeat this process for two sets of 12 times without causing any harm because the only weight that is moderately heavy needed.

This exercise will work on your glutes (muscle that runs along the back of your thigh which can extend the legs) and glutes. You can do this for two sets with twelve adverse effects since the only requirement is moderate weight. The golf squat is an opportunity to relieve the lower part and lower back of golfers. It is made to replicate the way that a golfer is holding the club in a game of golf. It builds strength on shoulders, and even on the back. If this is achieved the golfer can develop an amazing swing, with the highest level of impact.

Golf squats are an alternative to the lower part of the golfer. It is made to mimic the way the golfer is holding the club when playing golf. It builds strength on shoulders and even back. If this is achieved the golfer can develop an amazing swing that is high impact. Take three sets of twelve rounds with dumbbells and be sure to exercise both sides of your body to ensure that the muscles are balanced. While you work out, make sure to carry the leg exercises, you should not cause any disturbance. This will also give increase in the strength that you swing. Do this exercise for 30 seconds at a stretch, switching the direction you move. Three sets of 30 seconds are sufficient. It is suggested that you incorporate this workout with your core/abs workout.

The basics of Iron Play

Increase your score by re-educating yourself on the most important aspects in the swing of iron. Perform three sets of twelve rounds with dumbbells. Remember to exercise both sides of your body to keep the muscles in balance. As you carry out the leg exercises, you should not cause excessive disturbance. This will also give boost to the power that you swing. Do this exercise for 30 seconds at a stretch, switching the direction you turn. Three sets of 30 seconds are sufficient. It is suggested that you incorporate this workout with abdominal/core exercises. Increase your scoring by re-acquainting your mind with the essential elements of the iron swing. What's the point of an obscene 300 yards when you're unable to hit the green with your second shot? It's not worth the effort. Skills are always important in the event that you be professional golfer. The skills you have are more effective in improving your iron game. The ability to score well is due to sophisticated putt. It is also a result of properly hitting your approach shots close to the hole. Excellent drives are the result of more accurate shots that can result in lower scores.

The ball, the skills will always be important in the event that you become professional golfer. The skills are more effective in improving your iron game. The ability to score well is due to skilled putt. A good putting style also comes from the correct placement of your shots near the hole. Good drives are based on more accurate shots that in turn result in lower scores. Making sure your iron game is in good condition is the main base of your game. The bend should be originating from the waist, but not from the back. This creates a great posture. The golfer should grasp the club using his arms but not their wrists throughout the course of taking it away. The bend should originate from the waist, but not directly from the back. This results in a good posture. The golfer must pick up the club using his arms, not the wrists during the course of taking it away. A bad setup can't be excused as one must recognize the differences between a flawed setup and a properly designed one. As a basketball player flexes his muscles, which are well toned, and their knees are positioned on the ball with a solid posture, this could happen to golfers who wish to achieve professional status. This position of the leg aids during the backswing and downswing. The back must maintain its straightness, but not rigid.

The spine should be bent towards the ball, and the angle is maintained throughout the impact. In addition, the angle is felt in the hips, with the stable appearance to the left, but not at the waist.

A bad setup can't be excused as one needs to be aware of the distinction between a flawed setup and a properly set up one. Like a basketball has its well-toned muscles, and knees sit confidently on the ball with a solid posture, this could happen to golfers who want to be a professional. This position of the leg aids during the back and downswing. Your back should maintain its straightness but not rigid, and the spine should be positioned to the direction of the ball. The angle is maintained throughout the impact. The angle, more importantly, is located in the hips, with the stable appearance to the left, but not on the waist. Also, one should take note of the position of hands. They should be on top the ball, and if they are not, to the side of the ball. Be aware that the left arm is an extension to the shaft.

Do not try to play two different types of golf simultaneously That is to say when you're competing to win a medal, do not engage in a hole-to hole match with your opponent. You'll be confused and have no idea what you're trying to accomplish, and you'll most likely lose neither the medal nor the game. If you believe that you need to be in some way to the player who will be playing round with you, make sure you back your net return in comparison to his. If you complete make a hole with bogey or sometimes even with a single stroke don't think that you've played flawless golf. Certain bogeys are easy, and others are extremely sloppy. One could be unable to hit his drive, slam into through a bunker, then make a hole with his mashie, overcoming his bogey by one stroke. However, he is advised to not talk about it afterward to avoid being requested to give more specifics. The least amount of credit is given to him for this amazing performance. Always begin your swing at a low tee only when the wind is in your face. Be sure that your head is in a straight line from the time that you've taken the position you want and are ready to take your swing, up until you've hit the ball. When you address, always make sure to oppose the ball the part of the of the club you intend to strike it.

Ball Position

Then, let's talk about ball position. The most neglected aspect of the iron setup is the placement. The ball shouldn't at any time be placed away from the breastbone as many amateurs who prefer to move it further in the forward direction. Keep a golf ball close to your breastbone, while taking an ordinary stance over the ball. The full cock of wrists is when your hands are high above the shoulders. This keeps them from hanging from the front when taking off. If your shoulder forward drops the weight isn't moving in the right direction onto your hind foot in the backswing.

Keep your eyes at the other edge of the ball particularly when you're near the hole, or perhaps taking an occasional chip shot toward the hole. The tendency this point, [Pg 174) because of the stress of a golfer to be aware of whether they are lying dead or otherwise, and to shift eyes off of the ball and focus your attention towards the pin prior to the downward swing is completed and the stroke is executed. However, I don't approve of keeping your eyes focused on the spot where the ball was, in order to ensure that the grass can be visible after the ball has left. Keep your eyes at the ball till you've struck it, but not longer. It is impossible to follow through by hitting a long shot when your eyes are fixed to the ground. The ball is hit, and then let your eyes take it back at the speed as it is possible. This requires skillful timing and control, but the precision will soon become routine.

A Few Rules for Golf Competition

1. For Stroke Competitions, the competitor who finishes the course with the least number of strokes will be declared the winner.

2. When the lowest score are recorded by more than two participants the tie or ties will be determined in a different round scheduled for that same day. However, if the Green Committee determines that to be impossible or inexpedient they will then decide the next or a subsequent day when the tie or tie-breakers will be determined.

3. The holes are designed to accommodate Stroke Competitions after which prior to the start of the competition, no player will play on the putting greens or intentionally to play on any hole nor the putting greens in the event of disqualification.

4. Each hole's scores should be recorded by a specific marker or participants noting their scores. The scores that are marked must be declared at the end of each hole and at the end of each round, the cards must be recorded by the marker under penalty of disqualification and then handed back. The competitors must be sure before they hand in their cards they have their score for every hole are properly recorded, since no change

is permitted on any card once it is returned. If it is discovered that the score returned is lower than the one is actually recorded, the player is exempted from the competition. To add the scores recorded, by the secretary or deputy will be the responsible person.

5. If a player is playing beyond the boundaries of the teeing-ground, their penalty is disqualification.

6. If a ball gets lost (except in the circumstances provided for under the Rules of Golf), the player is required to return as close as they can to the location from where the ball that was lost was hit, tee a ball, and forfeit the penalty stroke. The ball that is lost shall remain in play if it can is discovered after the player has hit another ball. The punishment for a violation of this rule is exclusion.

7. If a player's balls hit him, his clubs or caddie, then the penalty will be one stroke.

8. If the balls of a competitor strike the other player as well as his caddies or clubs

or his caddie, it's an "rub off of green" where the ball must be played in the direction it rests. If a ball of a competitor that is in rest, gets transferred by another player or his caddie, or by his ball or club or by an outside agency, other than wind, it must be returned as close as is feasible to the location that it was lying without penalty.

9. A golfer must hole out using his own ball at each hole, with the possibility of disqualification. However, if it is discovered that he did not hole out before striking off from the next teeing-ground or if the error occurs on the final hole, after he has handed over his card and hasn't holed out using the ball he own, he will be permitted to come back to hole out with his own ball without penalty.

Chapter 18: Preowned Golf Equipment A Perfect Option

If you're on a profitable venture, golf can be your choice, and therefore there are many options for purchasing used golf equipment. From used golf equipment that has been meticulously cleaned to golf cars that do not fit the requirements of other golfers There are endless methods of finding fantastic but under-appreciated golf gear. Additionally, by giving a minimal amount of notice to the likelihood that you're not employed There are many opportunities to find a high-quality hitting on the fairway and earning an income from playing golf. Golf clubs are the most amazing part of every golfing pleasure. Finding used golf clubs may be unreliable, however there's endless options of the items you can purchase at golf shops. If you're cool, and you've thought about what type of golf clubs would fit you and resales that provide affordable prices to assist in purchasing high-quality golf clubs. If you are looking for left-handed golf clubs , or other amazing items that you can't resist, you'll be amazed by how easily your main goal for used clubs will be met with stunning outcomes. It doesn't matter if you're playing a game that is based on cash or prefer to spend your hard-earned cash on used golf clubs, there's no end to the possibilities and the options are awe-inspiring. Shoes that are worn but not damaged aren't necessarily an issue to purchase. They can be found in a yard sale thrift store, an existing store for golf enhancement and other stores, various brands of golf as well as other golf accessories are an obvious purchase. This is where the word "stability" can be an excellent tool to search for the items you are seeking in these stores. There's a saying in the resale shops that says, "That if you are searching for something in particular it is likely that you will not find it until after you've purchased the item new." A broad perspective is an excellent thing to have when you visit these resale shops. Golf balls that are used can be purchased in shipping containers or in thrift stores. They're a good purchase and meet an extraordinary need , allowing the golfer to practice his or her golf swings for a low price. Tee sacks are readily available at a minimal price too.

Golf towels, ball washers and projection wrenches are readily available on resales. Golf clubs and various accessories are important in yard sales as well as in resales shops. Golf vehicles and trucks can be bought even if they were previously used. The trucks that can be manually pushed are available with only effort for a reasonable price. Golf trucks are another option to add to your inventory of used golf products and taking charge of your pocket. There are firms that manufacture new parts for mechanized Golf automobiles at a price. However, purchasing an automobile that requires some minor repairs or some other mechanical component is an amazing option. purchasing used products is an excellent method for managing your money and usually you'll find high-quality and reliable products. There are occasions when there are some guards that are protected to think about. Therefore, you won't be spending your hard-earned cash on something that can make you look embarrassing on the course while at the same time, you are making money. Additionally, the pre-owned or exchanged advance asserted golf equipment, if it is highly sought-after will not cause you to be embarrassed in the long run when you are an expert golfer.

Seven Iron - The Perfect Club

Anyone who has watched the movie "Tin Cup" which focuses on Kevin Costner, will understand what the significance of the 7 iron - the ultimate golf club. The golfer is able to play a standard shot on the most part any course using the seven iron as well as a putter, in essence. In reality driving with a 7 iron will not give the golfer drives of 3 hundred yards, but on contrary it was never designed to strike the ball this far. Whatever junior golfers are an amazing shot when using the seven iron is achievable, up to striking one hundred and seventy-five yards up to two hundred and a quarter of a century.

The Seven Iron

If you are taking the drive using an iron seven, golfers should take the approach shorter. With respect in length to that of an opening the golfer could either force to swing full force or cut their swing. So the ball travels at a speed which isn't very beneficial for the golfer. In addition, depending on the conditions of the course and division golfers may have to position the ball the front on his foot. This gives the ball more room or maintain it at a lower level after the shot is made.

The Seven Iron

When the golfer is on the green the seven iron can be employed as a wedge to smash the ball off the green. By closing the position and then kicking the ball backwards of the hole the golfer is able to flip and knock the ball away from the green. It's clear that the golfer must reduce the swing or the ball could be thrown off the green and could result in a lost stroke or perhaps an unintentional loss of ball. When the ball is chipped into the green the convenience of the seven iron is at a minimal level unless the golfer exhibits remarkable courage and wishes to use the seven iron to putt. This, too, was performed in "Tin Cup " film. In essence the typical three openings. The seven iron is also the best club to use. In the long term the golfer could start teeing and hit from the front or back of his or her spot. However, this depends on the distance in which the ball can be placed higher to allow for more area and less. In fact, it creates an discord having both feet on the ball of golf, however, it prevents the golfer from taking the most out of his swing, and also from flying over through the green.

The iron will, however it is, allow the ball to be struck higher and with greater control. In addition, a properly hit seven iron is a thrilling experience to see. The ball launches in a spectacular round, following a planned flight plan, and then flies spectacularly across the sky before landing gently on the grass. It helps golfers move closer to achieving his final goal. Seven irons are also beneficial to keep in the home, since it's length is sufficient for a player to achieve his goals.

A Few Heating Ups

This is the most effective time to warm up when three or four golfers are able to strike the drives with everything they can. Actually warm-up forms can bring satisfaction since it's believed as meaning that you'll be able adjust your swing to play great golf. Also, you will be able to adjust to conditions of the weather even if temperatures rise more than when it's cold. The process of warming up can be superior than the usual methods of preparing to begin playing golf, however, it must be executed in a planned manner.

A Golfer Warming Up

Choose the iron you will start with during your few drives , which will allow your muscles time to ease off. In the event that an athlete is injured on the knee or lower leg, the driving iron could be utilized as a stick permitting the player to walk back to their hotel or to the nineteenth hole to have a drink. It is evident that there are moments when nothing is working and the golfer is forced to put the club away and focus on the issue. Driving seven irons are the best to correct this flaw since it's a golf club that is very broad in its method of striking the ball.

Online Golf Tips and Tricks

Tips from online sources can aid in strengthening your golf game and increase your golfing performance. So, these tips from the web can be a great help for every golfer. From experts to novices all golfers have a drive desire to be a good golfer along the course. Additionally you'll be motivated to achieve your goals. Through the help of golf online, you'll be able to see numerous qualities that stem with the information you find on the web. You'll see on the messages sheets and in the net journals that individuals from every kind of background are eager to share their tips during the game of golf. These tips will guide even the most promising set of players. Once you have registered with the club as golfer, you'll build relationships and gain knowledge by interacting. Some clubs have launched an update program for golfers with the latest news and exciting stories on

Chapter 19: Golf Swing

There is software that can enhance your game. In terms of recognizing your golf reorientation the form and technique of your swing could be obviously the most essential aspect that you can concentrate your game. There are a variety of educational segments and programs available to all who want to help you master a golf swing. It is possible to gain by having your technique and swing analyzed. After examining each of the crucial elements that are essential to having a successful golf problems, your swing can be eliminated. The most effective method to improve your game is to develop an entire swing is to study your swing and your style.

A golf swing test can be improved with most recent programming available or programs that have been in use for a long time and has been proven repeatedly, resulting in an unrivaled swing of all sizes and shapes for golfers. No matter if you're a enthusiast of golf or a weekend warrior golfer, the programs for golf swings will assist you in determining the areas the areas where your swing is getting a bit sloppy. In addition, you'll be able to improve your golf swing to ensure that your maximum potential is realized at the golf course.

A Great Posture

With the most cutting-edge technology available in the field of setting up your golf game, there's no reason not to join the professionals. With a bit of determination and some effort you'll be able to begin to love your golfers with a child-like affection. Whatever way an individual golfer is playing there is one thing everyone will appreciate is that having a harrowing day playing on the fairway is better than the most productive day working. It is important to start with golf as an job. You'll pay little attention to how confusing the game might be once you start to play along the course.

A Great Posture

Golfers are aware that although each shot might not be a spectacular thing however, they are still poor and shouldn't be a cause for concern. Also they will appear identical to the shots professional golfers shoot on television. Work is what everyone has to be doing to stay alive. When we wake up in the early morning with a large portion of us worried about what lies ahead then get focused and set out for our place of business. It doesn't matter if it's a getready office or a plant work place, it's the occupation that keeps us in our place. Work is a striking four-letter word. Work is where the issues are discovered. The managers are required to assist in addressing the issues or else they'll be forced out of working. Although unemployment could allow a person more chances to go golfing however, it doesn't offer the opportunity to pay their bills or get food items to eat.

The workplace is also where the boss is and many individuals haven't grasped the importance of work and do not use the correct techniques to profit from it. There are managers who must motivate employees to work and make sure that the boss is aware of the requirements of those who are under his supervision. Three or four bosses may create programmes for the golf of their bosses in the various clubs they belong to.

However, there is a different type that includes directors who are not as reliable. They don't have any input or have the ability to say anything special to their respective staff members. They always complain that the club isn't making money, and paying little attention to what the assessment sheet of the club states and be a petty nuisance for everyone else who is around them. This is not the basis of the game in a sport like golf. In golf, there's no boss on the course. A man's occupation or social arrangement doesn't matter on the fairway.

The most important thing everyone examines is the manner in that he plays effectively and whether he is able to have the ability to play at a reasonable pace. In golf it is common to hit the fairway. an acceptable strategy to reach an agreement with your fellow players and to meet new people.

Golf is just a few feet from all-too-short path for one man to get over the disappointment. The feeling of hitting a golf ball is odd, and the better the ball gets hit, the greater the acclaim the golfer receives and pays not a lot of attention to whether he/she is playing with a partner. To bring it into the issue, which golfer hasn't smashed an entire ball before, stopped, observed the ball fly by, considered and said, "Man, that is an amazing shot!.

This way, the skilled golfers playing on the fairway accomplish more than the average worker would be able to accomplish in a single day.

Golfing in the Wind

The weather conditions have a major influence on golf, particularly the winds. A wet golf course will hinder the ball from moving as much the way one wants after the impact of being struck, the wind can negatively impact the performance of a golfer's game. The wind has a greater impact on the play of golf than any other circumstance. What could be the reason? Based on the present circumstances First, winds can affect the direction of the ball, moving it away from the normal course of flight and dropping it in a place the golfer didn't anticipate the ball would go.

A Golfer playing in the Wind

The golfer should be aware of the direction in which it is winding and also be aware as to how steady it's being blown. Naturally, if winds are blowing across the fairway, it will not significantly affect the strategy of the golfer, and also his confidence. In this scenario the golfer has to leave a footprint as the ball is pushed higher and the wind completes its job, especially in the direction of the ball. When the player is on the tee box with the wind blowing strong so that the play of golfers could eventually be affected. If the golfer is trying to strike the ball directly to the flag, he'll be astonished to see the ball being diverted into the opposite direction from the causeway. A slight angle to the green, the ball completely disappear from the green, causing an attempt at a chip shot there, without hitting the target and not hitting the usual. The fast golfer will think about the force of the wind and the method of taking the shot. A professional golfer is thus, able to put off on an eighty-seven-yard three hundred and eighty normal four-hole course with a powerful wind blowing mostly directly in their direction. The most amazing idea is for the golfer to alter their position and to keep the ball in a low position and away from the wind. In this way the golfer can take an ordinary swing. The golfer should take into consideration the angle of the shot, by setting his or her position to keep the ball in a low position. Additionally, it's similarly an excellent idea to choose a club one time more than he would normally do. In this case, if the golfer is using an iron with seven holes to cover the final one hundred fifty yards using a an extremely difficult course and a challenging, he must think about making use of a six or five iron.

Making the Ball Go to the Right Place

The art of hitting the ball properly isn't an easy feat. Golfers must be aware of their swing and think about the dynamics of a ball that is stationary. Similar to base ball players, who hit the ball straight, and travels with a high speed as well, golfers has to master the art of golf. Because of this, those who are new to golf engage in the game of golf in the hope that their game will begin to develop with only a little effort. It is important to review many of those players who quit playing golf before they achieved mastery in hitting that golf ball. It is amazing that iron clubs can hurl the ball for in a few yards with a flurry of imagination occasionally. There's much more involved in hitting the tiny ball than what is apparent to the naked eye.

Look at the club and find it located on the back of the club which makes it simpler to identify the right club to play golf. When the golfer attempts to master their swings, they must to make sure that the club has a firm grip on the surface of the golf club with the floor. This is why, when you take everything into consideration that the ball does not move, or more accurately, it moves in the opposite direction. Instead of trying to hit the ball the ball up, you must think about your downswing. If you strike the ball downwards the club will follow the path of your arms, not the upward movement of the club.

If you do an downswing that edge pushes the golf ball forward. It's the center of your golf ball. However getting the force behind that tiny ball is a matter of practicing. You'll be enticed to swing huge and powerfully, but remember it takes as much effort to resist that urge as it does to learn what to do with the ball. Once you've set your self up for an upward swing, you'll see that the ball and it starts to increase in size. From the beginning, you'll begin to be aware of the various golf clubs, and the choices you'll need to make before making shots. You'll need to choose the club you want to use and then utilize its edge to strike the ball, and then observe how far it travels and the direction it travels. If you've mastered your game but think you don't have the confidence or grasping the game Ask for assistance. Your fairway should have experts who will provide you with a few tips.

A Fairway Green

You might consider taking private lessons. The shop that is the course master should have suggestions to local teachers. However, you can try the massive old friend method. If they have any suggestions for hitting the ball could be great for you. It's possible that you'll think you're absurd, but once certain golfers begin to impress you with their tales of understanding how to make the perfect shot, you'll have made progress in your golf game. If you follow these tips and maybe a few tips from magazines on the internet and websites, you'll have improved in your swing. It takes time to train your brain to recognize the downswing and not the upward swing. It takes time to get your body set to execute it the right way , which is the main goal. Take whatever steps you need to take to not give up your game. Golf is a sport that will. It takes the time to learn and particularly when you are striking the ball.

Conclusion

You may surpass 90.

Do you believe the sentence above? Do you think you've got what it takes to make it into the 80's for the very first time, and to repeat the process repeatedly? If you're not convinced you're capable You might want to quit right now, since you're not going to be able to do it. Golfing requires faith in yourself people who are doubtful about their ability aren't going to be successful on the course.

Once you've got confidence in yourself as part of the puzzle Once you have that, you can start working on your game making use of the tips that have been included within this guide. It doesn't take a pro golfer to make it to 90 - it's just a matter of being constant, follow an established game plan and be able to implement the plan on the golf course. There will be holes that are not perfect on the way however that's part of of golf. Do not go out hoping for perfection on the day when you finally reach 90. Instead, set out with the intention of hitting the fairway first. When you have reach the fairway, you can proceed for the second shot, and then execute it to the best of your ability. So long as you remain to the 'shot-by-shot mental approach throughout the course, you'll be able to avoid the pressure that may often hinder the process of achieving a new personal top.

I hope you've been able to leave reading this article with drive and information you require to reach 90 the very first time. The most exciting aspect of trying to break a record in golf is that you can never stop at a different goal after the current one has been achieved. If you achieve sub-90, establish a new goal and work hard to reach it well. There is no one who has ever mastered golf and nobody ever will. Always strive for new goals and milestones and this amazing game never gets old. Have fun and be successful!

Thanks and best of luck!

www.ingramcontent.com/pod-product-compliance
Lightning Source LLC
Chambersburg PA
CBHW050403120526
44590CB00015B/1811